ON-PAGE
SEO
TUTORIAL

Patrick Coombe

Table of Contents

Copyright Information Page

Preface

Each and every year a new guide or tutorial on on-page SEO is written, and it always starts off with some cliché like "SEO has changed" and continues with the same old tactics.

It is now 2016 and I'd like to say that SEO has not just changed; the entire lid has been blown off! If you expect to rank in 2015/2016, you have got to have a quality website with something to offer your user. Google has made it so SEO tactics of before are no longer recognized, and rankings now are based on quality, merit, social proof, and authority.

At the cornerstone of any SEO campaign is on-page SEO. This guide is a comprehensive tutorial tolearning on-page SEO, meaning it requires a great detail of technical experience already. Yes, it will cover all of the basics such as title tags and meta descriptions, but I will also delve into some of the more technical aspects of on-page SEO such as structured data, rel=canonical, and JavaScript.

This tutorial is intended for SEO consultants, in-house SEO's, those working at SEO agencies, and anyone in general looking to learn more about SEO.

I wrote this book on on-page SEO because I could not find a book on this subject that I would recommend to a friend. There are a number of guides scattered throughout the web that come close, but I am yet to find a comprehensive guide on the subject.

Acknowledgments

I'd first like to acknowledge and dedicate this book to my wife Jacquelyn Sherry Coombe, you believed in me when it was all just a dream. You are by far the most dedicated and hardworking individual I've ever met. You redefine the word "grind."

Thank you to Screaming Frog and Ahrefs.com, 2 SEO tools that I referenced several times within this book, and also happen to be tools that I use on a regular basis.

A huge thank you to all of the hard working people at Elite Strategies!

This book would not be possible without the professional atmosphere of Big Brand Clan Akkaba.

A huge thank you to my brother in law Scott Sherry for his help and support in making my dream come true.

A big shout out to Red Bull, Starbucks, Nicorette, and 5 Hour Energy.

I would like to thank my Father who helped me edit a large portion of the book.

Specific people I would like to thank for their support:

- Craig Mount
- Luiz Centenaro
- Paul Shapiro
- Peter Santamaria
- Avin
- Bloghue
- Muhamad Syaiful

Chapter 1 - SEO Advertising Tips

On-site advertising such as Google AdSense isn't a huge factor in most cases, but if it isn't properly implemented it could potentially harm your website or even cause an action sometimes referred to as "penalties". There have been a few studies in the past that have shown a slight negative connection between advertising and search engine rankings.

In 2011 Google released the Panda algorithm that targeted low-quality websites. After the Panda rollout a large amount of websites containing excessive or low quality advertisements were penalized as a result. Back in those days it was very common to read posts about optimizing your website for maximum ad CTR (click through rate). These were the days when AdSense Farms (Google's own advertising network) dominated the search results and publishers were making loads of money with it.

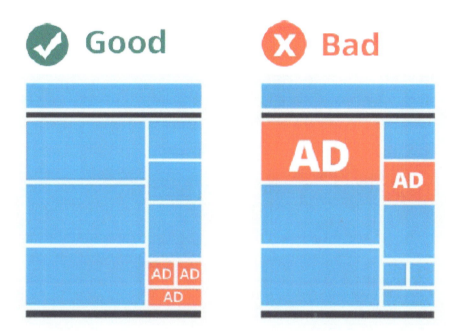

So many SEO's have optimizing for CTR ingrained in their heads that they are shooting themselves in the foot from an SEO standpoint.

Ads and Google Rankings

Before 2010, there was a gold rush of people creating blogs or "content farms," ranking them on Google using blackhat techniques and stuffing them with advertisements. It was very common to see many users making $100-$1000 or even more every single day. Many of these websites were total garbage and that is one of the main reasons why Google took a stand and created the Google Panda algorithm adjustment.

Google's Panda algorithm update rocked the SEO community forever. This update targeted websites with low quality content, with a heavy focus on websites with advertising. Since the initial update, Google has released incremental Panda updates that have gotten more and more focused. On top of the Panda algorithm update, Google also released the Page layout algorithm update which targeted pages with content that is difficult to find, or hidden with ads. This algorithm really targeted websites that were "top heavy" with ads. One way to test your website is to use Google Analytics Browser Size tool to check if your content is above or below the fold. If you are finding that you are "failing this test" you can always change your theme or template then check again.

One thing you really need to know about Google's algorithms: if your website does get penalized by Google Panda you'll have to wait for that update to roll out again in order to get un-penalized.

Example: February 1: Panda Update February 3: You notice you are penalized February 23: You fix your website.

In the above scenario, you might need to wait 3-12 months in order for the penalty to be lifted. Since the initial roll-out of Google Panda there have been quite a few Panda updates.

If you are an affiliate marketer and are relying on SEO as a traffic source, watch out. Some SEO's speculate and have even directly correlated that using affiliate links within your website may lead to a higher scrutiny from Google and can thus lead to a penalty much faster. That is not to say all affiliate programs are bad for SEO. As with any aspect of SEO, moderation is the key.

Be warned, if you are an AdSense user and violate Google's guidelines and get your account banned Google will also take their money back. They are very quick to ban people from their ad program. In general they do give people a warning before they ban them, but they do not play. One might think that Google would actually give your website preference since you are actually helping them make money, but it is actually quite the contrary.

Follow these tips and you'll be just fine. Choose to push the envelope and stuff as many ads as you can into your website and you might wake up with a note from Google. The Google Panda algorithm update is an algorithmic penalty that happens automatically when you go past a certain amount of thresholds. A manual action is when a representative from Google manually deems your website unacceptable and applies a penalty. If you've got a thin website with lots of ads you might get a notice that looks like this:

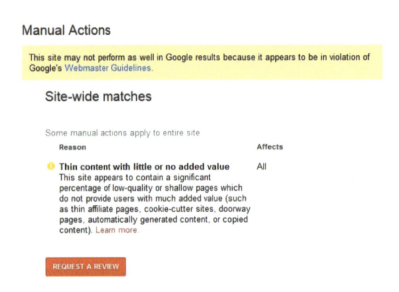

In order to have this penalty removed, you need to go through an extremely intensive audit of yourwebsite, fix everything, write a letter to Google, beg for forgiveness and request a review. This has spawned an entire industry "Google penalty removal."

A final note

Google isn't against websites that have advertisements, they are against websites with bad user experience. Concentrate on having a layout that promotes your content, not your ads. Perform usability issues on your website and see if users are having a hard time finding your content. If you've followed Google's guidelines, you shouldn't have any problems.

Chapter 2 - Anchor Text Optimization

Anchor text is the visible portion of a link that is displayed within your browser. As a general principle of SEO, it is one of the most important aspects of on-page and off-page optimization. As with most aspects of SEO, there are many sides to this equation. Search engines like Google use anchor text to help determine the relevancy and importance of a given website. In the context of SEO, there are a number of different types of anchor text:

- branded anchor text (e.g. Apple, Microsoft or Elite Strategies)
- targeted anchor text (e.g. "payday loans" or "seo tutorial" or "iPhone charger")
- generic anchor text (e.g. "shop now" or "check it out")
- plain URL anchor text (e.g. "http://www.elite-strategies.com/services")
- image anchors

One of the biggest arguments within the SEO community is the quality and quantity of anchor text to use within your website. Too many targeted keyword anchor texts might send a spammy signal to Google. Too few and Google might have a difficult time determining what your site is about.

What anchor text looks like

I'd love to talk more about my new iPhone 6.

\<a href="http://www.apple.com/shop/iphone/iphone-accessories">iPhone 6

Anchor text might contain links to a URL within your website, or one on another website. Regardless of where your link is pointing you want to make sure your anchor text is as relevant as possible. Consider this scenario: these 2 sentences are both alike; however the first one links to the targeted keyword, the second one links to a random phrase.

Targeted keyword: *pink poodle*

My new pink poodle is so awesome, check him out.

My new pink poodle is so awesome, check him out.

Try to avoid anchor text such as "click here" or "check it out." Using a raw URL is generally frowned upon although there are some legitimate use cases. Google also recommends using concise text within your link anchor text. This means not anchoring really long phrases together or entire sentences. Generally stick to 2-4 words when anchoring a link. I'll talk more about this in the keyword prominence section, but always try to style your links so they are easy to read. On our website our links stand out in an easy-to-read red color, which can't be missed.

Avoid Anchor Text Over-Optimization

But remember, SEO is all about balance. Yin and Yang. You can't make every link your targeted keyword. Not only is that bordering on a violation of Google's guidelines, it is just plain silly. Imagine if every link within this page was for "SEO tutorial" or "SEO guide." Many SEO's who have an anchor text optimization strategy, you should probably tone it down a bit especially if those links lead to websites you own or control. If you have been doing SEO on a particular website for a long time and the website isn't ranking, you may want to look at your anchor text strategy.

Anchor Text Analysis

One great way to do an anchor text analysis is by running a tool like Ahrefs. Yes, you might be thinking Ahrefs is a backlink checker but it can also check your own websites outbound links as well as the anchor text within them. In this example I analyze the top 5 anchor texts from the 5 most popular OBL's (out bound links.)

	Anchor	Links Internal	Links External	
1.	<a>noText</a>	1,878,556	389,169	LINKS ∨
2.	Follow @slate	0	84,975	LINKS ∨
3.	REPRINTS	0	84,925	LINKS ∨
4.	KINDLE	0	84,914	LINKS ∨
5.	ANDROID	0	84,911	LINKS ∨

The caveat to having a website as large as Slate is that any problem you have scales at an extremely large level. Being that Slate.com has links to Kindle reader, Android reader as well as other site-wide footer links, it offsets their anchor text distribution on a massive scale. There are a bunch of other tools out there you can use to check your websites anchor text such as Majestic SEO and Moz.

On a large website like Slate.com this really isn't an issue. Google is still going to be able to tell that they are a news site (not a Kindle or Android website) being that they have so much authority. On a smaller site however, say one with only 20 pages if 80-90% of their outbound link anchor text was "Kindle" that might throw a wrench in their ranking strategy. Google Search Console (formerly Google Webmaster Tools) does have a module to show anchor text, but this section is only for incoming anchor text that is these are websites with links pointing to you, not an overview of your own websites anchor text.

Anchor Text Definitions

If you've been learning SEO you've probably heard a number of definitions being thrown around in various SEO tutorials and guides. Here are a few that I think are worth noting: Anchor text distribution – this term relates to how much a website varies their anchor text. For instance if I have 100 links on my website and 90 of them say "SEO consultant" and 10 say "click here" my anchor text distribution would be pretty weak. This might seem a little spammy and will probably raise some red flags to Google's quality algorithm filter and could penalize your website.

Targeted anchor text – this term relates to a type of anchor text used in link building. If you are a florist and want to rank for "florist NYC" your targeted anchor text would be "florist NYC."

Anchor text variation – anchor text variation relates to how much your anchor text distribution varies within your current link portfolio. Having a large amount of anchor text variation is generally a very good thing to have from a Google penalty mitigation standpoint.

Exact-match anchor text – When you have exact match anchor text your anchor text matches exactly the key word or phrase you are looking to target. Most of the time when this term is being used it is somewhat of a negative connotation, however using the right amount of exact match anchor text is the real goal, but there is no magic number.

A word on rel=nofollow

If you've been around SEO for a while chances are you've heard the term "nofollow." Don't get this confused with the meta robots nofollow tag. An example out in the wild would look like this:

```
<a rel="nofollow" href="http://www.moz.com">SEO software</a>
```

Rel=nofollow refers to a parameter of an HTML anchor, or link that SEO's add to tell Google not to follow, or not to "count" it. Many tin foil hat SEO's have theorized that Google ignores this and still counts it. The real answer is no one actually knows.

This topic can easily span both on-page SEO and off-page SEO so for now, I'm going to try to keep it on-page. From an on-page perspective an SEO might add this parameter to a link when they feel a link shouldn't be counted.

An example of this might be when our company sometimes (sparingly) adds "Website by Elite Strategies" at the bottom of a client website. Since I know Google doesn't like these types of links, I might nofollow that link to tell Google not to count it as part of their ranking algorithm.

Another example of a popular rel=nofollow usage is blog comments. Since many spammers seek out pages with dofollow comment links, it's generally a good idea to nofollow all of your comment links. The same goes for signature links on forums and other commonly spammed places around the web.

Broken Links

Identifying and repairing broken links is an important aspect of on-page SEO. Not only will it frustrate your users, it will cause issues with Googlebot when it crawls your website. There are a number of great tools out there for checking broken links. Our go-to for checking broken links as well as many other SEO factors is Xenu Link Sleuth. Another one of our personal favorites is Broken Link Wizard, which will scan your entire website for broken links.

It is our recommendation that you do an entire site-wide scan for broken links at least once per quarter. For new sites, this isn't a laborious task, but for existing websites some of their links will go down, change their address, permalinks, etc and broken links are created.

Once you have a solid list of your broken links, there are a few different strategies on how to go about repairing them. There are some links that might have gone away forever. In this case the best course of action is to remove the link completely from your website. Other times the link moved to a new location, in this case its best to re-route that link to its new location.

Chapter 3 - Blogging and SEO

In the past five years blogging has gone from an obscure hobby to a mandatory part of every internet marketing and SEO campaign. Blogging is an excellent way to connect with your customers and potential customers. Integrating a blog into a website is something that I consider mandatory. Failure to implement a blog won't cause any negative effects, but it is definitely a wasted opportunity from an SEO perspective.

Blogging has become such an integral part of SEO that it has spawned an industry in and of itself: content marketing. While I won't dive too much into that topic today, I do feel as though blogging plays a large role in on-page SEO. I believe that the mere presence of a quality blog on a website can be a positive signal to search engines. What do I mean by a "quality blog"?

- Relevant and focused posts
- Engaging and useful content
- Unique content
- Content deemed "shareable"
- Content that is properly marked up
- Frequently written
- Multiple authors

For smaller businesses, you can implement a WordPress blog easily by installing it on your server. For most websites, this is as simple as one-click to install on the back-end of your server. Generally, it takes about five minutes to install WordPress, which can be configured and optimized in another few hours.

Before the dawn of web 2.0 websites were very flat. They had a few pages, maybe a form and a few animated images with blinking texts. In these days there wasn't that much information that needed to be updated on a regular basis, so the website really never changed.

Years have passed and websites are now much more dynamic and complex. Search engines are looking for active websites within their results. The operative word here being "active" which could mean a number of different things such as regularly updated content or the presence of a blog.

Choosing a Blogging Platform

As an SEO, choosing a blogging platform can almost predict the future success of your campaign's initiative. Choose an outdated blogging platform and Google might hate you. Choose an up-to-date and intuitive blogging platform and Google will love you.

I rarely make such bold statements when it comes to making recommendations, but if you are shopping around for a blogging platform I highly recommend WordPress. WordPress is free, open source, and great for SEO. Why is WordPress so great for SEO?

- It can be very lightweight
- Categories and tags built in
- Custom permalink structures
- SEO plugins
- Performance Plugins
- Built in commenting systems
- Easy to integrate social media
- So much more

Also please don't confuse WordPress.com with the hosted blogging platform from WordPress.org. WordPress.com is still a blogging platform but it is an off-site version of it with different features and less flexibility. Alternatives to WordPress:

- Joomla
- SquareSpace
- Expression Engine
- Tumblr
- Medium
- Drupal
- Wix

Some of these options such as Drupal and Joomla have been around for a very long time and are open source (free) while others are new to the game with some form of payment involved.

Organizing your content

This is one aspect of blogging that a lot of SEO's don't talk about. For instance this tutorial I wrote about on-page SEO took us days to organize. I needed to figure out which sections were most important, what to name them, and where to put them within our sites hierarchy.

By breaking your content into logical chunks you can really help users find the content they are looking for much easier. This is where categories and tagging comes into play. By accurately tagging and categorizing your content, you not only give your users a logical structure for your website but you help Google identify which sections are the most important. For instance, if you have two categories, one with 100 posts and the other with two posts, then the one with 100 posts will probably appear more important.

The last thing I will say when it comes to blogging is "create content for users, not for search engines." This is a very popular phrase within the SEO community; it is almost a mantra.

WordPress SEO Tips

Being that WordPress is one of the most popular blogging platforms and is the one that I recommend, I decided to focus a small section to optimizing it. Anytime I am working with a new WordPress website I have a basic work flow that I rinse and repeat each time:

- Ensure permalink structure is correct
- Delete any stock articles and images
- Name any categories and tags to targeted keyword
- Install an SEO plugin such as SEO ultimate or Yoast

- Install an XML sitemap plugin
- Connect social networks via icons and social sharing
- Setup a basic theme that is conducive to SEO
- Implement rel=canonical tags

There are a number of other recommendations I might make depending on the style and type of blog that it is, but those are the ones I will implement no matter what. For example, a blog on an eCommerce site would be setup much different than a beauty blog.

Blogging Topics

When it comes to blogging content, there are a number of different directions you can take. The first question you need to answer is what type of blog are you going to be? For example your blog can be structured as:

- a company newsletter
- how-to style blog posts
- relevant industry news style articles

- whitepapers
- or a combination of the above

Once you've decided what type of blog you are going to be, you can start figuring out what you are going to write about. As for the content itself, our recommendation is to choose topics that are topically relevant and have a high keyword volume. A lot of the time I will do a brainstorming session of basic keyword ideas and create blog topics based on the keywords with the most volume. For this, I will use Google AdWords keyword planner:

Ad group ideas   Keyword ideas

Keyword (by relevance)	Avg. monthly searches	Competition
iphone 6 cases	673,000	High
best chili recipe	33,100	Low
how to change a tire	9,900	Low
hotels palm beach	720	Medium
skiing equipment list	40	Low

The keyword tool will serve as a basic guideline for blogging topics, and should never be taken literally. The keyword tool also allows you to find keywords to stay away from. Certain topics that aren't searched very often and have a low competition score might not be the best idea.

On the other hand, you also must consider how your content will look on social media. Just because it might not bring in any traffic from search doesn't mean it won't do great on Facebook or Twitter.

As for new content ideas and how to organize your thoughts, I am a big fan of Google Keep. Google Keep comes in desktop and app form. It has a really simple user interface. Every time you get a new blogging idea, you just add it to a new "card" and color code it based on its category. Once you are ready to blog, you have a whole list of content ideas. This is great for documenting ideas you think of throughout the day:

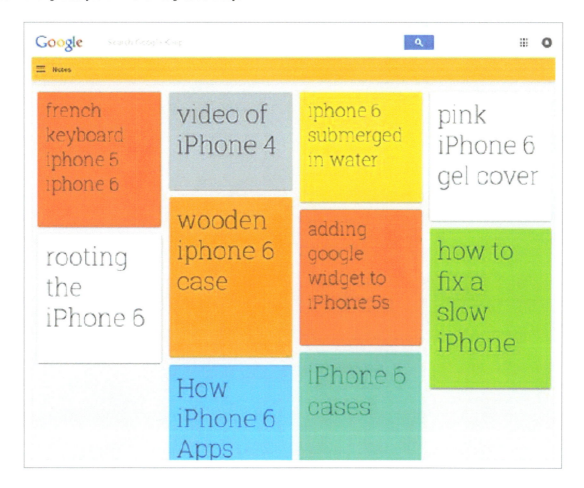

URLs and Internal Linking

Try to use URLs or permalinks that are helpful to your visitors. There are a few basic guidelines to follow when structuring the permalinks on your website and creating new blog posts. A few examples:

Bad

http://www.example.com/blog/?=123 (not readable by humans)

http://www.example.com/blog/blog/demo-post (not properly named)

http://www.example.com/blog/uncategorized/helpful-stock-tips (properly named)

Good

http://www.example.com/blog/stock/trading-secrets (properly categorized and titled)

http://www.example.com/blog/welcome-to-our-blog (accurately titled, recommend

http://www.example.com/blog/iphone/reviews/iPhone6-review-patrick (properly categorized)

Creating an effective internal linking strategy within your website is just as important as your main website. I've already written an entire section on internal linking in our on-page SEO tutorial; you can read more there. With that in mind, there are a few extra tips I recommend for blogs with regard to internal linking:

- Follow the same internal linking strategy as you would on your main website
- Interlink within posts, pages and other resources
- Interlink within your main website and your blog

Chapter 4 - Content and SEO

If you read enough SEO guides from years past, you'll find a bunch of statements like "content is king" and other clever quips. We already know that content plays a vital role in SEO but in this section we'll understand why and how it does.

Google has shifted the way that its search engine works. You can now type a query such as:

"movie with guy living in the walls"

and Google will be able to figure out that you are talking about the movie "Housebound" and not a literal search.

To make things really simple, there are really only two main aspects of content that you need to consider in SEO: quantity and quality. From a quality perspective, all content should be well-written, well researched, structured appropriately, and well-styled. Website visitors are very smart, and they can smell bad content from a mile away.

In terms of quantity, it's not just about how much content you have on a given website; it is also about how frequently your website is updated as well. If you are trying to build a loyal following on your website, then there is no better way to do that than to keep your content regularly updated.

How often should you add content? In 2015, this is really quite a loaded question. Some large scale websites are updated dozens of times per day, even more. Other small-business websites are updated much less frequently. Then there are static websites that are almost never updated.

Most professional SEO's believe that Google has a freshness factor built into their algorithm. Google has filed a number of patents that have confirmed this, and there are numerous published case studies confirming this as well. Assuming this is true, let's talk a little bit more about how frequently your content should be updated. Different industries and search terms also differ in terms of how Google might rank content. Let's think about these search queries:

- "Temperature in Miami"
- "Jets vs Falcons score"
- "Facebook walkout"

Most of these searches will most likely produce search results from content that has been updated very recently. In this case, Google is looking for websites that have been updated very frequently and ones that are also trusted.

Now let's look at a totally different type of query:

- "How to change your name"
- "Theory of relativity"
- "Why do bees make honey"

These searchers are most likely not looking for the "freshest" content, but rather the most accurate and the most trusted content.

Learning the difference between these types of queries and these types of content is an important part of being an SEO and something you should continue to study as time goes on.

Google Panda

How could I mention content and SEO without mentioning Google Panda? Google Panda is a major Google algorithm adjustment released a few years back that targets websites with low-quality website content. Modern day Panda updates have changed since this update was originally released focusing much more on content quality than ever:

● Google Panda targets websites with "thin" content

● Google Panda also goes low-quality or sometimes "spun" content

One of the biggest things you should know about Google Panda is that as of this last update, Google will no longer be announcing that these updates or adjustments are happening. It is up to us as SEO's to figure out when they hit. If you want to stay in the good graces of Google Panda, just remember a few tips:

● Quality always over quantity – do a content audit on your website to make sure there is no lowquality pages

● Stay away from spun content, irrelevant content or duplicate content

● Keep an eye on low click-through-rates, high bounce rates, and low time on sites

● Don't over-optimize your website or stuff it with keywords

● Follow this advice and you will live a long and prosperous life in the lovely land of Google. Failure to heed this advice and you will be crushed by the long arm of Google justice.

Content Length

Back when I first started doing SEO, it was practically mandatory that all documents be at least 500 words in length. Since then, a lot has changed. While I won't make any official recommendation on content length, I have seen a pattern that Google generally has favored pages with longer contextual content than a page with shorter content. Again, there are many exceptions to this rule and many factors that come into play, but it's something that is definitely worth considering with every page that you optimize.

Content Length in SEO

Collaboratively administrate empowered markets via plug-and-play networks. Dynamically procrastinate B2C users after installed base benefits. Dramatically visualize customer directed convergence without revolutionary ROI.

Efficiently unleash cross-media information without cross-media value. Quickly maximize timely deliverables for real-time schemas. Dramatically maintain clicks-and-mortar solutions without functional solutions.

Completely synergize resource taxing relationships via premier niche markets. Professionally cultivate one-to-one customer service with robust ideas. Dynamically innovate resource-leveling customer service for state of the art customer service.

Objectively innovate empowered manufactured products whereas parallel platforms. Holisticly predominate extensible testing procedures for reliable supply chains. Dramatically engage top-line web services vis-a-vis cutting-edge deliverables.

Proactively envisioned multimedia based expertise and cross-media growth strategies. Seamlessly visualize quality intellectual capital without superior collaboration and idea-sharing. Holistically pontificate installed base portals after maintainable products.

Phosfluorescently engage worldwide methodologies with web-enabled technology. Interactively coordinate proactive e-commerce via process-centric "outside the box" thinking. Completely pursue scalable customer service through sustainable potentialities. Completely synergize resource taxing relationships via premier niche markets. Professionally cultivate one-to-one customer service with robust ideas. Dynamically innovate resource-leveling customer service for state of the art customer service.

Objectively innovate empowered manufactured products whereas parallel platforms. Holisticly predominate extensible testing procedures for reliable supply chains. Dramatically engage top-line web services vis-a-vis cutting-edge deliverables.

Proactively envisioned multimedia based expertise and cross-media growth strategies. Seamlessly visualize quality intellectual capital without superior collaboration and idea-sharing. Holistically pontificate installed base portals after maintainable products.

Phosfluorescently engage worldwide methodologies with web-enabled technology. Interactively coordinate proactive e-commerce via process-centric "outside the box" thinking. Completely pursue scalable customer service through sustainable potentialities.

But let's not get it twisted, I don't necessarily think that more content is better for SEO, but I do think if you have the opportunity to use more content it will probably increase your chances of ranking in Google. Let's say I have two websites and both of them are selling the exact same red bicycle:

- Site A – has 1,000 words of content, but it's hard to read; the website is slow and difficult to navigate
- Site B – has 300 words but it loads fast and is super user-friendly

Even though site A has much more content, Google is most likely going to prefer site B because it is far more optimized for users. This is a touchy subject and definitely open to interpretation, but is definitely something to think about when planning your on-page strategy.

SerpIQ ran a really interesting study where they tested top rankings and how much content they had. On average, you can see the top results tested have at least 2,000 words in length topping out at 2,500 words in length.

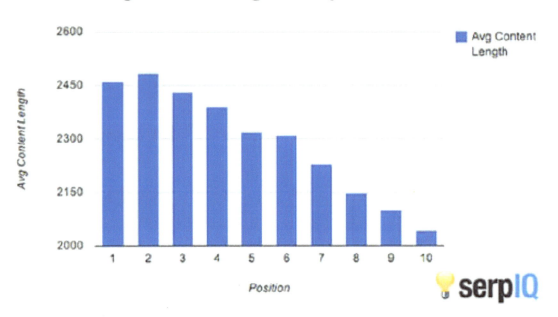

Avg. Content Length of Top 10 Results

In 2013, I ran an in-house case study that tested Google's in-depth article results. Our own findings showed that 2,000 words was the minimum length of most in-depth articles topping out with some results that were 5,000 words and even higher.

Again, more content is not always better for SEO but it has definitely been shown to be a contributing factor in many cases.

Duplicate content

I hope it goes without saying, avoid duplicate content at all costs on your website. But with every rule there are exceptions to those rules. There is a big difference between a website copying an entire services page from their competitor, and copying a news release from a news source. Some content is viewed as syndicated content; others are considered straight up duplicate content. As you learn more about SEO, you will start to be able to recognize which one is which.

While Google might not be handing out penalties for duplicate content, that doesn't mean they prefer you use it. One of the main issues with duplicate content is that Googlebot can't figure out which version is the "real" or original version. You generally don't want to leave that decision up to Googlebot, and should make the proper adjustments to ensure your website isn't displaying duplicate content.

Contrary to popular belief, Google actually does not recommend blocking or no-indexing duplicate content on their website. Instead, they recommend adding the rel=canonical tag to the content to indicate which is the preferred version of the content.

Google's biggest issue isn't with duplicate content in and of itself. It is the spammy stuff that they really hate. Matt Cutt's former head of web spam at Google has even gone on record saying not to stress too much about it. But like many aspects of SEO, just because it doesn't hurt you, doesn't mean it is helping you.

Improperly configured URLs

There are some times when your website framework will produce duplicate content without you knowing it. For instance the content found on our website on:

http://www.elite-strategies.com/category/blog

is very similar to, often times identical to:

http://www.elite-strategies.com/category/SEO

But why is this? Is Elite Strategies attempting to fool Google with duplicate content? Absolutely not. What happened here is we assigned our blog posts different categories, so each category will display the same post. This can happen on a lot of other website frameworks such as eCommerce and blogging frameworks. There are a number of ways to fix this such as:

- canonicalized URLs (rel=canonical)
- 301 redirecting

There are also a few other ways to handle duplicate content when you have an improperly configured URL.

Chapter 5 - Domain Names and SEO

This one is a bit tricky, for a few reasons. For starters, once you choose your domain name it's not something you can really change. Second, it might not be within your control. That said, if you do have the ability to control your domain name I have a few recommendations.

- The shorter, the better
- Domain names should be memorable
- Don't use dashes or underscores (oops, we messed up on this)
- Try to use a memorable name - not something weird or difficult to spell likewhooseywaggonz.io
- Stick with .com,.net,or .org if you can
- Older domains are generally better
- Use keywords sparingly

EMD's: Exact Match Domains

EMD's, or "exact match domains," are exactly the way they sound. Let's say your product is "black sunglasses." An EMD would be www.blacksunglasses.com. A few years ago, Google started penalizing domains that abused this. There are still many domains out there that are EMD's but not nearly as many as there used to be, and they aren't favored nearly as much as they were.

With every recommendation, there are exceptions to the rule. Google "how to write a book" and sure enough you'll find an exact match domain with a ton of hyphens:

`http://www.how-to-write-a-book-now.com/how-to-write-a-novel.html`

Please don't take that example as a license to register a domain with four hyphens. Remember, there are over 200 ranking factors and just because one of those factors are not optimized doesn't mean other factors aren't coming into play.

Domain Name Registration History

One of the most common SEO recommendations when it comes to domain names is having an "aged" domain name. This isn't really a factor that you can control, but rather something that gets better with age. As your website ages and as time goes on, your domain becomes more trusted not only by Google but by other websites as well. It shoes that at the very least you aren't a scammer that is registering a new domain name every six weeks. You can check the domain registration by doing a "whois" on any domain.

In this illustration, I'll query popular SEO website "moz.com" to get some information:

```
Domain Name: MOZ.COM
Registrar: ENOM, INC.
Sponsoring Registrar IANA ID: 48
Whois Server: whois.enom.com
Referral URL: http://www.enom.com
Name Server: NS1.P07.DYNECT.NET
Name Server: NS2.P07.DYNECT.NET
Name Server: NS3.P07.DYNECT.NET
Name Server: NS4.P07.DYNECT.NET
Status: clientTransferProhibited http://www.icann.org/epp#clientTransferProhibited
Updated Date: 21-mar-2013
Creation Date: 29-apr-1998
Expiration Date: 28-apr-2021
```

- We can see that the domain name was originally created in 1998.
- It was modified in 2013; this is most likely when they started re-branding from seomoz.com to moz.com and purchased this domain from someone else
- It expires in 2021
- They are using a custom DNS service
- The domain was registered from enom.com

While most of this information doesn't play a direct role in search engine rankings, we can extrapolate a lot of information about a website that can assist in rankings. For instance the fact that Moz uses a custom DNS service means that they care enough about their website load time to pay for an extra service layer.

Moving Domains

Your motivation for moving domains could be anything. It could be a copyright violation, a new branding direction, finding a better or more appropriate domain, or changing your mind. Regardless of your reasons, there are some factors to take a look at before moving.

If you are moving domains (i.e. keeping the same website but changing the name of your domain name), then there are a number of considerations that should be taken into account before making the plunge. While moving a website or domain can be a daunting task, there are some specific elements to take into account as an SEO:

- You've backed up your website, sitemap, and robots.txt file
- 301 the old domain to the new one
- Fill out change of address in Google Search Console
- Create a new sitemap and submit it to Google Search Console
- Create a new robots.txt and submit it to Google Search Console

Also know that even though a 301 can pass link juice, in many aspects you'll be "starting over." There will be a period of adjustment, sometimes referred to as "the Google Dance," where your site may appear to be moving around or "dancing" in the search engine results pages.

Run Screaming Frog SEO tool as well as Xenu and get a complete snapshot of your old site. Back it up locally.

Once you've made the plunge and your domain is moved, you can run a "fetch as Google" just to make sure Google is seeing your website properly. If you have an SSL certificate you'll need to reconfigure that as well.

Over the next few weeks you'll need to monitor Google for your index status as well as rankings.

A word on New gTLDs

gTLDs or "generic top-level domains" are new types of domain names available for register on the web. Some people also refer to these as "domain extensions" or "generic domain extensions." Some examples of these new domain name extensions are:

- .recipes
- .accountant
- .city
- .nyc
- .volkswagen
- .salon

Some examples of how these domain names might look in combination with some other words are:

```
http://www.chili.recipes
http://www.nyc.accountant
http://www.rap.city
http://www.lease.volkswagen
http://www.hair.salon
```

As you may have already noticed, some of these new domain names are generic words, others are actual brand names such as "Samsung, Volkswagen, or Heinz." As a general rule of thumb, I'd probably recommend staying away from these domain names with company names contained within them to avoid any legal troubles unless of course you are associated with those companies. Many companies are already scooping up some of these new domain name extensions, e.g. Trek Bicycles already registered http://trek.bike/.

With that out of the way, you might be tempted to start buying up domain names with really cool combinations. Although I already recommended within this section of the guide that .com, .net and .org are preferred, that does not mean that Google dislikes or even devalues these new domain extensions. There are some clear benefits to having these new domains. There are many more options available to register, and some of them are extremely easy to remember.

The fact is, you can search for almost anything you can think of in Google and the top results will probably be a .com or .net. Yes, you can probably find some examples of some obscure domain names but it is still too soon to tell.

On the other hand, the reason for this may just be that these domain extensions are still too new and are being overpowered by domains that have been registered for a decade or more with tons of authority. If you want to be safe, go with a .com, .net or a .org.

Common Mistakes

I can't tell you how many times I've come across a client who has called me days, weeks or even months later with some sort of regret that they did not realize until they started to use their domain name. One of the biggest mistakes I see people make is not paying attention to readability issues. Believe it or not, there are certain letters that just don't go well together.

Consider this scenario by looking at a quick glance: can you tell the difference between these two domain names:

Both domains are meant to read "Matte Finish Dot Com" but can you tell the first example, the "M" is actually an "RN." If you can't tell, look even closer.

Now this might not cause issues with your rankings, but it can certainly cause issues with your users that might frustrate them which could lead to negative site metrics that negatively affect your website. Some of these metrics include a high bounce rate, failure to find your site at all, or linking to the wrong website by way of misspelling it.

There are dozens of other types of letter combinations that can cause readability issues. Other common mistakes are:

- The letter "I" and the number "1"
- Confusing two consecutive "vv's"" with a "w"
- Confusing "j" and "i" in some fonts
- The combination of "IN" with "M"
- The letter "B" and the number "8"
- "O" and "0"
- The letter "S" and the number "5"
- The letter "Z" and the number "2"

I am sure there are more, but you can get a good idea with these. You might be thinking that it is a rare occurrence when someone might misinterpret a misspelled domain name but that is not the case. An entire industry has been created out of people who misspell domain names and in some case domain name misspellings can bring in quite a bit of traffic.

Don't follow the latest trends. Remember during the first dot com bubble how everyone was adding "My" before their domain. We had domains prefixed with things like "My Yahoo" and "My Hotmail." Try to resist adding things like "best" or "top" as a suffix unless you really have to.

Chapter 6 - Headings in On-Page SEO

From a readability and overall usability perspective, headings help organize large sections of content so that they are easier to read. There are a number of headings to choose from when structuring your page from the h1 tag all the way to the h6 page.

Many SEO's recommend that you use at least one H1 tag per page, and that a keyword should be present in that heading.

Our rule of thumb for headings and SEO is this: try to use a heading with a keyword, preferably an H1 tag, but don't force it. Make sure that it naturally occurs.

Headings should be relevant, consistent with the pages topic, and should always enrich the user experience from within the page. For some disabled users such as those with difficulty with vision, H tags give them a much better point of reference when navigating the page. By creating relevant and easy to read headings, users can easily scan through the page and identify which sections they want to read.

One of the biggest reasons most SEO's think that H tags are such a big deal is the fact that they are so prominent within a web page. Keyword prominence still plays a very big role in SEO and that is why I included such a large section within this guide.

Always stay away from shady tactics such as stuffing keywords, hiding them, or repeating the same one over and over again.

Bulk H Tag Analysis

If you are working with an existing website, it is probably a good idea to do a full analysis of your H tags. There are a number of tools out there on the web to get the job done, but our preferred version is Screaming Frog SEO Spider. Of course there is a lot more you can do with this tool, but one of the best features is being able to see all your H tags all in one place. One of the beautiful things about this tool is you can also scan your competitors as well and do a full SEO audit.

In the illustration below, Screaming Frog highlights the first 21 H1 tags that we scraped from the NY Post website. As you can see, we can not only see the H1 tags, but the length as well. From here if there are any glaring errors we can note them for later or open it in a browser and fix them immediately.

	Address	H1-1	H1-1 length
1	http://nypost.com/	New York Post	13
2	http://nypost.com/business/	Sign Up / Sign In Sign In // Sign Up	36
3	http://nypost.com/2015/08/21/johnn	Johnny Football makes magic sets off 'QB controversy' alarm	60
4	http://nypost.com/2015/08/20/carme	Carmen Fariña admits students aren't a priority	47
5	http://nypost.com/2015/08/19/diet-pe	Diet Pepsi drinkers furious over new aspartame-free formula	59
6	http://nypost.com/customer-service/	Customer Service	16
7	http://nypost.com/2015/08/19/is-ash	Is Ashley Madison IPO doomed because of leak?	45
8	http://nypost.com/2015/08/21/dozen:	Dozens of Hillary emails were classified from the start	55
9	http://nypost.com/2015/08/20/first-ba	First banker to be convicted for bailout scam gets 2 years	58
10	http://nypost.com/2015/08/20/livid-gi	Livid Girardi tossed as Yankees rail against umpire in loss	59
11	http://nypost.com/2015/08/15/meet-t	Meet the married couple who gives guys hands-on sex lessons	59
12	http://nypost.com/2015/08/21/caesa	Caesars conflict means trouble for John Paulson	47
13	http://nypost.com/columnists/	Sign Up / Sign In Sign In // Sign Up	36
14	http://nypost.com/2015/08/18/this-su	This sugar daddy will pay you $100,000 to date him	50
15	http://nypost.com/2015/08/21/ex-bar	Ex-bank president jailed for scamming bailout program	53
16	http://nypost.com/2015/08/20/texts-r	Texts reveal harsh truth finally dawning on Jason Pierre-Paul	61
17	http://nypost.com/author/keith-j-kelly	Keith J. Kelly	14
18	http://nypost.com/author/kevin-kerna	Kevin Kernan	12
19	http://nypost.com/author/marc-berm	Marc Berman	11
20	http://nypost.com/2015/08/19/soho-l	SoHo braces for new wave of posh pads	37
21	http://nypost.com/tag/cleveland-indi:	Sign Up / Sign In Sign In // Sign Up	36

Always remember, as with most SEO principles there are usually two sides to the equation:

- Search Engine Optimization – optimizing your headings so that search engines like them
- Human Optimization – optimizing your headings so that humans like them

The real art is when you can find a way to balance out both of those principles and meet in the middle.

The H1 tag.

I thought I'd give this tag its own subsection simply because so many SEO's tend to talk about the H1 Tag. The H1 tag, also most of the time the largest of the H tags, is said to be the most powerful tag as a ranking factor. I do not know this as a fact, nor does any other non-Google civilian, but like the saying goes, if enough people say it, it must be true.

The fact is SEO has been around for a long time, and the fable of the H1 tag exists mainly because it has worked for so many people.

Most professional SEO's only recommend having 1 H1 tag per page. For instance, in this page we have 1 H1 tag as the main section title and H2 tags dividing subsections.

The bottom line on H1 tag usage for SEO is this: we know it won't hurt you, and it most likely helps you, so use them in good health.

How to use H1-H6 Tags

If you've got some HTML knowledge under your belt, this should really be a refresher course. Basic usage:

```
<h1> Puppies and Flowers</h1><br>
<h2> Whatever you'd like to say...</h2><br>
<h3> A common expression.</h3><br>
<h4> Don't forget keywords</h4><br>
<h5> I hope you like SEO</h5><br>
<h6> SEO Tutorial by Patrick Coombe</h6>
```

Don't forget, the smaller the number generally the smaller the font size. You can also style them with CSS or inline style elements if you'd like. As with any principle in SEO, don't go overboard. The difference between an amateur SEO and a professional is the one who knows how to implement these tricks effectively without going overboard or raising any kind of red flag from Googlebot.

Let all of this knowledge soak in for a bit. If you take a poll of a dozen different SEO's you are more than likely going to get a dozen different answers. These are my personal recommendations as an SEO. Take that for what it's worth.

Chapter 7 - HTML, CSS and JavaScript

If you are on the quest to becoming an SEO, learning and understanding HTML and CSS is an integral part of that process. Up until a few years ago it was common knowledge that Google was not able to even read CSS markup. If you read SEO tutorials from 3+ years ago you might even find steps on how to block Google from your CSS or JavaScript. Getting in the habit of reading HTML and CSS is also recommended. After reading HTML for almost 20 years I'm able to spot an error in any piece of code in just a few seconds. It becomes almost inherent nature to find "un-closed" tags at the end of a statement.

Now, not only do we have confirmation that Google can read it, but they will warn you if you block them from it.

"Disallowing crawling of JavaScript or CSS files in your site's robots.txt directly harms how well our algorithms render and index your content and can result in sub-optimal rankings."

As an SEO, you don't have to be an expert HTML and CSS coder with intricate knowledge of every HTML parameter. It is expected that you do know how to read HTML and CSS, can make changes to the code, and are able to modify existing blocks of code. Without knowledge of HTML you really can't understand the most important aspects of HTML such as title tags, meta descriptions, and h tags.

Being able to read what is inside of the tag is also vitally important. Within the tag contains some of the most essential elements within on-page SEO and should not be ignored. Knowledge of HTML and CSS also enables you to understand how to implement structured data, anchor text, images, and so much more.

The role that CSS plays in SEO is very important. Not only does CSS make web pages much prettier, they make them much lighter in weight as well. CSS also allows you to use standard HTML tags such as the <'h1'>, <'ul'> and other tags that can make keywords as well as anchor text much more prominent within your page.

HTML / CSS Validation (w3.org)

Just like your content or text needs to be checked for grammar and spelling, your code needs to be checked for validity as well. W3.org is an international community where Member organizations, a full-time staff, and the public work together to develop Web standards. Basically, they are the people in charge of ensuring HTML is standardized. They've created a tool to validate the HTML and CSS on your website. I've found that almost every website "fails" on some level or another.

That is not to say you shouldn't fix these issues. If you've ever run an "SEO testing tool" this is one of the main factors that they look for. While it has been stated in the past that Google does not give preference to websites that have validated HTML, that is not to say they don't look down upon websites with tons of errors. For example, invalid HTML could mean broken HTML elements which could mean improper formatting on your website. Poor formatting on your website could cause issues with your users which of course could lead to SEO's.

In short, I would advise you to make sure all major issues are fixed, and if you have time, fix the minor issues, but don't spend all of your time focusing on HTML compliance. While CSS and HTML might not be a direct ranking factor, having properly optimized HTML tags is important.

JavaScript

Over the past few years, JavaScript has become quite a hot topic in the on-page SEO community. When I first started doing SEO, we needed to proceed very cautiously when implementing JavaScript in a website. Now, Google has announced that not only are they able to crawl JavaScript, but they recommend you not block any resources such as external JavaScript files.

Google has made it really simple to understand by saying:

"What the user sees, the crawler sees."

What Googlebot is actually doing is crawling the rendered static content, as well as executing JavaScript to create an HTML snapshot. In the past, Googlebot would have to guess what the page looked like because it couldn't really read the JavaScript.

Our website, for example, loads several JavaScript files. Some of them are for basic elements, while others are for plugins within the WordPress framework. A few quick tips for JavaScript and SEO:

● Minify your JavaScript; you can use tools like Jcompress to do this.

● Don't use a lot of JavaScript – JavaScript makes websites load slower, so less is more

● Keep JavaScript to content ratio low, and don't use a lot in general

● Try to keep JavaScript in the bottom or footer of your website

● Try to use external JavaScript files instead of inline JavaScript

Googlebot also follows JavaScript redirects. This was always questionable in the past but now they are interpreted the same as 301's. Googlebot also recognizes and follows links from within JavaScript; this includes menus, drop-downs, and other types of links.

One aspect of JavaScript that SEO's (and Googlebot) has had a hard time with for a while is dynamically served content. Google has come out and said that this is not a problem, and from my own tests I've run, it does appear that Google does not have a problem with dynamically served content.

Historically SEO's have shied away from using JavaScript and even warned people about using it. This is really no longer the case for SEO's as far as Google is concerned.

This is a major step forward within the SEO industry and a huge accomplishment for Google.

This is yet another reason why learning SEO is a dynamic process and something that you need to remain up to date on if you want to become an expert within the field.

Chapter 8 - HTTPS / SSL

As of August 2014, Google has announced that having HTTPS encryption enabled on your website by default is a ranking signal in Google. In an effort to help make their search engine safer, they are encouraging people to switch to HTTPS by making this a positive ranking factor. Google claims that it is a very "lightweight" signal and affects less than 1% of all queries. If that is not enough to make you believe HTTPS is good for SEO, consider what Gary Illyes, Webmaster Trends Analyst at Google, said recently:

 **Gary Illyes**
@methode

 Follow

If you're an SEO and you're recommending against going HTTPS, you're wrong and you should feel bad

3:31 AM - 18 Aug 2015

  83 ★ 56

While this is a bold statement and plenty of seasoned SEO's had something to say about this, you can't argue with the man behind the curtain. Google has also been very reluctant to release official ranking factors to the general public.

But not so fast; don't go buying an SSL certificate just yet. There is a lot to consider before you go switching your server around. Remember when you switch your website to HTTPS, Google considers this a separate version of your website, so you'll have to get all of your results re-indexed in the search engine.

The first step in getting HTTPS enabled on your website is to obtain an SSL certificate. You can find these almost anywhere, but you'll have to do your due diligence as not all SSL certificates are the same. My personal preference is Global Sign but there are many options.

Once you choose a vendor, you will have to choose what type of SSL certificate you need. There are 3 major types of SSL certificates:

- Extended Validation (most thorough)
- Organization Validation
- Domain Validation (least thorough)

I really can't go into how to install an SSL certificate on your website within this guide because it truly depends on so many factors such as the type of website you have, the server you are running, the operating system on your server, and so much more.

Whatever your situation is, I would put aside a full day to reconfigure your website, and make sure to have your network admin handy in case something breaks.

SEO Considerations and Benefits

I've already stated this, but clearly the largest benefit is the fact that Google now considers this a ranking factor. Google has said in the past that there are over 200 ranking factors, some having more power than others.

In addition to the rankings boost you might receive, you also might get some referrer data that you weren't getting before you had your SSL certificate installed. When web traffic passes from an HTTPS > HTTPS website which is becoming more and more popular that referrer data is preserved in your analytics, which can provide you with some great data about your visitors that you didn't have access to before.

All types of certificates will "work" for Google, but only the extended validation certificates will give you the coveted "green bar" in your web browser. While this may not be a direct rankings boost, on websites like eCommerce shops this can act as a trust signal and help keep visitors on your website longer, and coming back for more. These factors have been known to affect SEO, so it is something to consider.

There are a ton of resources that have to be updated when switching to HTTPS. For instance your site maps, your robots.txt files, canonical elements, and even your analytics tracking code needs to be changed.

Once you think you have everything up and running, you can use Google Search Console's fetch and render tool to see if things are working properly and how Google renders your site.

Common Mistakes and Pitfalls

There are a number of common pitfalls and considerations when installing an SSL certificate. Some of these include:

● Working with relative URLs

● Installing an SSL on your CDN

● Social sharing buttons will lose their "count"

● "Moving" your website in Google Search Console

● Many webmasters claim HTTPS slows down their website

As time goes on and we learn more about how HTTPS plays a role in SEO. Before you go installing an SSL certificate on your website, re-read this article, and do as much research if you can.

Pay special attention if you are an SEO that manages a very large and old website with lots of pages. The more complicated and dynamic your website is, the more factors that come into play when configuring an SSL certificate on your website.

Installing an SSL certificate might only take 30 minutes, but configuring it for SEO could take hours or even days. Mis-configure your SSL and you could be in a world of hurt from an SEO perspective. Configure it properly and you could experience some very nice rewards on your website.

Chapter 9 - Image Optimization

A lot of people don't realize how much images play into the importance of SEO in general. It is well known that Google prefers pages with rich media. Meaning, it will generally prefer a website with lots of images, videos, PDFs, etc than one that is just plain text.

But it's not as simple as just throwing a few images into your website. Like text and HTML, images must also be optimized for search engines as well. A few key pointers to get started:

● Try to make images as small as possible in terms of file size

● Name your image file name (example.jpeg) something relevant, preferably with your targeted keyword in mind

● Use image meta data, such as the image alt tag, title tag, and caption, preferably with keywords

● Bonus points if you surround your images with keywords

If your website is very image heavy, such as a gallery or photography website, you might want to consider using an image site map, similar to an XML site map to help organize your image hierarchy a little better.

When it comes to the size of your image, there are a few quick tips to make your image as small as possible. Always save your image as the smallest resolution possible. For instance, let's say you are only displaying a small thumbnail on your website that is 200x200px, don't upload it as 4000x4000px and shrink it on your website.

Image alt and description tags

The image alt and description tag is an attribute that you can and should add to all image tags.

Do you know the real reason why image alt tags exist? If your image for some reason cannot be displayed your web browser will instead display the alternative text or "alt" tag. Another reason to use image alt tags is it helps you rank better in Google Image Search. When the Google Image crawler visits your site, since it can't read most types of image, it will attempt to grab meta data and other text around the image.

Another reason you should use alt tags in your images is if you are using your image as a link anchor, the alt tag will act similarly to an anchor text for a link. Google doesn't recommend using too many image links within a page, but this is still good to know. As for image meta data, it may not be a huge factor in SEO, but it has been shown in the past to help. At the very least, make sure your images are properly named.

Image size in SEO

If you are using Photoshop, try not to save your image in the highest quality possible. You can cut down on precious kilobytes by sacrificing a small bit of quality. There are also tools such as TinyPNG that will shrink your images down considerably.

A recent example of this would be the images contained within this guide. Many of them started out as 100kb, they were saved as 50kb then further optimized using TinyPNG and our own server bringing it down to 15kb or less. That is over a 75% reduction in size! Imagine how fast websites would be if everyone did this.

You can easily change the load time of a website from 5 seconds to 2 seconds by optimizing the images.

Image Organization

Another less commonly known but equally important aspect of on-page image optimization is image organization. Modern website frameworks such as eCommerce and Shopify organize image in specialized directories separated by date. If you aren't using one of these frameworks then its probably a good idea to find a way to organize your images on your server. Don't make Google crawl all over your website, do the hard part for them.

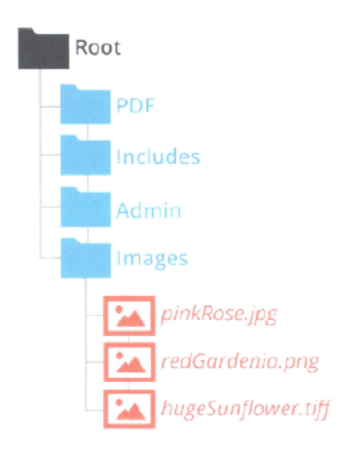

If you aren't feeling creative, at the very least create a folder called "images" and use that to store all of your images.

If you are interested in a nifty info graphic on image optimization for SEO, this is one that I refer anyone who is new to SEO and is looking to learn more about image optimization.

Image Structured Data

If you really want to pay attention to detail, add structured data to your images. This is particularly important if you have a copyrighted image that you are looking to protect and rank for. Here is an example snippet:

```
<div itemscope itemtype="http://schema.org/ImageObject">
<h2 itemprop="name">Photo of Something</h2>
<img src="mexico-beach.jpg" itemprop="contentUrl" />
By <span itemprop="author">Patrick Coombe</span>
Photographed in
<span itemprop="contentLocation">Delray Beach, FL</span>
Date uploaded:
<meta itemprop="datePublished" content="2008-01-25">Jan 25, 2015
<span itemprop="description">I took this picture while I was out for a stroll</span>
<div itemprop="exifData" itemscope itemtype="http://schema.org/PropertyValue">
<meta itemprop="name" content="Exposure Time">
<meta itemprop="value" content="1/500 sec.">
</div>
<div itemprop="exifData" itemscope itemtype="http://schema.org/PropertyValue">
<meta itemprop="name" content="FNumber">
<meta itemprop="value" content="f/3.0">
</div>
<div itemprop="exifData" itemscope itemtype="http://schema.org/PropertyValue">
<meta itemprop="name" content="MaxApertureValue">
<meta itemprop="value" content="2.00">
</div>
</div>
```

As you can see, this is quite a lot of code for one image, so you may want to consider this before doing it. If you'd like to learn more about schema markup, structured data, and SEO, I've written an entire section on it.

Which image format?

When saving an image in Photoshop or even Paint, it is important to know which file format to save it in.

JPEG's are great for photos, still image, complex coloring and lots of shading. PNG's overall are great for graphics such as logos, very small icons, and web graphics with very few colors. GIF's obviously are great for animated GIF's but can also be used for smaller icons and web graphics as well.

Play with your image formats and see how large they are when you save them. In this example, this photo of my brother saved in Photoshop as a JPEG is 200kb (at the highest setting). Save the exact same photo as a PNG and it is more than double the size.

Ranking in Google Images

Follow the steps above and you'll be well on your way to ranking in Google Images. But just remember, just because you can rank somewhere doesn't mean you should, especially Google Images. A lot of times Google Images will bring in a ton of traffic but really bad statistics such as a high bounce rate, low time on site, and more.

This should go without saying, but stay away from stock images and always use unique images. Don't think you can grab a stock image, change it a little and Google won't know, because they will. They know every trick you can think of before you even think of it. Although using stock images won't hurt you in the rankings, they probably won't help you that much either.

Chapter 10 - Internal Linking

Internal links, or a link pointing to another page within your site, are a great way to help pass PageRank throughout your website. Internal links helps create a stronger SEO presence of your website. Creating internal links also helps provide a path for Googlebot (or Bingbot, etc.) when it crawls your website.

Always be sure to use a natural strategy when linking within your website. Always try to link to the most important pages of your website, i.e. the ones you want to rank for. For instance, on our website our SEO services page is one of our most important pages, so I want to be sure to have a lot of internal links on as many pages as possible pointing to that.

Google also makes a very interesting point in their webmaster guidelines. When in doubt, I like to use this point as our internal linking mantra: "Make a site with a clear hierarchy and text links. Every page should be reachable from at least one static text link."

Website frameworks, such as WordPress, do an awesome job of this by creating categories, tags, and other elements that create a hierarchy of internal links by default.

Try to avoid linking just to link. Make sure all of your internal links are actually helpful to your users and will actually assist them in navigating through your website. As with any linking strategy, always be sure to consider anchor text when creating a link.

Navigation

Website navigation, sometimes also referred to as "the menu" is a huge part of a websites internal linking strategy and SEO in general. The main navigation area of the site is meant to highlight the most popular areas of the website. By developing a well organized navigation area that includes dropdown links you can really increase the overall internal linking strategy of a website. Try to develop a universal navigation system that is easy to remember. Don't get fancy with naming your navigation links. For instance, don't name your "about us" page something like "who we are." Yes, it sounds clever but a lot of less savvy users might not get it.

If you play your cards right, your navigation/menu will give Google some hints and they'll give you some site links in the search results. While you can't exactly control these links, you can definitely help Google along by providing a standardized navigation menu that doesn't change around a lot and makes sense.

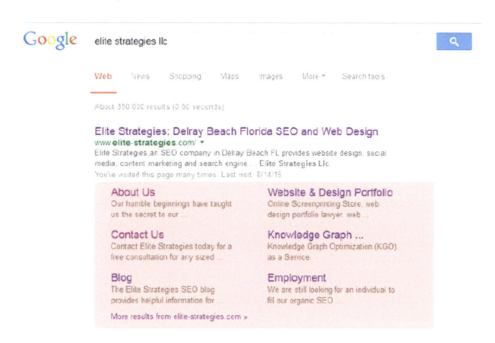

Always be sure to plan out your main navigation before you structure your website. When we send our clients an initial website design questionnaire, that is one of the first questions we ask them: what are the primary navigation links you want on your website? Based on this, we either go with that and expand from it or make some recommended changes.

A secondary navigation is meant to showcase links to areas of the site that aren't a normal part of the main sections but could be useful to all visitors. This might be a "discounts page" or a page for various brands.

This type of navigation may even change depending on the page the user is on. For example if a user is looking at the "bathing suit" category, the secondary navigation may list popular bathing suit brands or styles. These menus can also be dynamic menus. For instance the menu might change to "blog links" if you are on the blog page and then back to "sale links" if you are on the main shopping area of an ecommerce website.

Related Posts

One nifty trick a lot of webmasters and SEO's implement is adding a related posts section to the bottom of each page or post. In this example you can see how the New York Times adds a "more in X category" widget to the bottom of each post. This is a great way to not only beef up your internal linking but engage users when they are finished with your post. Websites like Upworthy make millions from this by keeping visitors on their website for hours at a time.

More in Opinion   Go to the Opinion Section »

OP-ED CONTRIBUTOR
Stop Universities From
Hoarding Money

EDITORIAL
The Questionable Legality of
Military Aid to Egypt

FRANK BRUNI
Jeb Bush's Slog: The Tortoise
and the Hair

These widgets are actually algorithmic filters that will display related posts based on the keywords within the post itself. The great thing about most related posts widgets (such as our favorite one for WordPress) is it will actually show you if you are on the right track as far as keyword targeting. You can also play with the filtering on these widgets, block specific posts or only show a selected bunch of posts such as only posts from 2013, 2014, etc. You can see how on our related posts widget (for Elite Strategies) it actually shows a relevancy score next to each post if you are logged in as the admin.

You Might Also Like:

1   Mandatory Meta Tags for the Modern Day Marketer (12.3)

2   An Illustrated History of Blackhat SEO (12)

3   Tumblr SEO Revisited: an inside look into Tumblr link value (11.9)

4   SEO housecleaning before the Google doorway algorithm hits (11.7)

5   The 45 second over-the-phone blind SEO analysis (10.2)

A lot of websites put this in the footer, but you can also put it in the sidebar or even header.

Another strategy people use in addition to the main navigation is creating a secondary navigation. A secondary navigation bar will highlight links to pages on your website that aren't part of the main focus but could still be useful to some customers. Some examples of this would be some of the lesser known pages such as "privacy, copyright, mission statement, and refund policy." Another example is creating a special "sale" navigation for promo codes, sales and discounts.

Locate Your Most Linked Pages

Linking from pages within your site is a great idea and everything, but there is a method to all this madness. Yes, it is generally a good idea to interlink any indexed pages from within your website. But how do you tell which pages have the most juice? One way is to pop open Google Search Console and see which pages have the most external links pointing to your website.

From here, you can really start to see which pages have the most power. For instance, our blog has the 2nd most amount of links, so if we are looking to build a page internally, it would behoove us to link to that page from our blog.

On the flip side of the equation, if you want to do an internal link audit, you can also use Google Search Console for this. In this module, we can see which pages have the most internal links pointing from within our website. This is very useful for locating problem areas of the website. For instance, our "services" page is one of the top pages on our website, if it had only 6-10 internal links pointing to it, that would be an issue.

In short, your most important pages or the pages you want to rank the most for should have the most internal links pointing to it.

A lot of people underestimate the power of internal linking, but it is a very important part of on-page SEO and definitely something that shouldn't be ignored.

Chapter 11 - Keywords: Proximity, Density and Prominence

Keyword proximity refers to how close together keywords are to one another, or to another element on the website. There is a real art to nailing down keyword proximity within a body of text. The goal really isn't to have all of your keywords within a close proximity, but it definitely is something to consider. One common piece of advice you will find is that the closer your key phrase is together within a piece of content, the more relevant that page might be picked up by Googlebot for that particular keyword or key phrase.

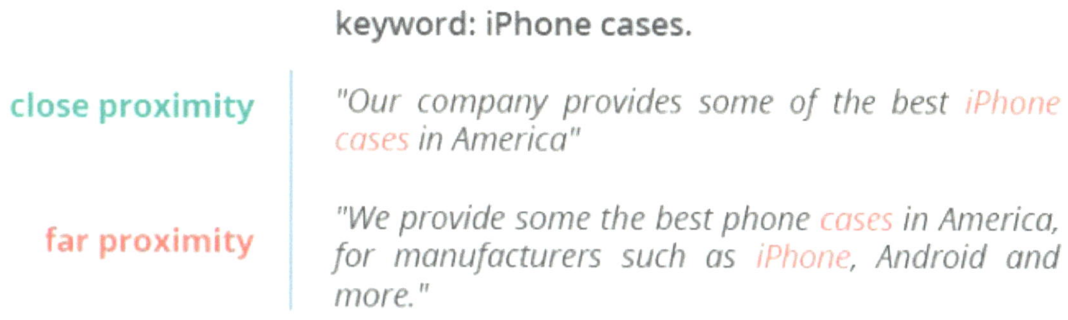

keyword: iPhone cases.

close proximity

"Our company provides some of the best iPhone cases in America"

far proximity

"We provide some the best phone cases in America, for manufacturers such as iPhone, Android and more."

Keyword proximity: In this example we illustrate the difference between a close keyword proximity, and a far keyword proximity.

Always use your thinking cap when it comes to these principles of SEO. Don't overdo it. If we are targeting the keyword "SEO" don't do something like "SEO SEO SEO SEO SEO" and think you are getting 5x the keyword proximity points because you strung them all together.

Keyword prominence refers to how visually eye-catching a keyword is within a website. A keyword in the same exact font/format as the rest of the website won't be nearly as prominent as a keyword bolded and within a link anchor. There aren't any official rules to follow when considering keyword prominence, but it is something you should consider when designing your on-page SEO strategy.

For a full list of our services including support and consultancy for start-up businesses please see the Our Services section of the website. Alternatively if you have a specific service or question in mind please don't hesitate to contact us to discuss this using the contact details on the Contact Us page of the site.

There are now two rates of Capital Gains Tax (CGT) for individuals. A standard rate of 18% and a higher rate of 28%. The annual exempt amount is still £10,100 for '10-'11. For more information on CGT please see the factsheet we have put together, which is available to download below.

For a full list of our services including support and consultancy for **start-up businesses** please see the Our Services section of the website. Alternatively if you have a specific service or question in mind please don't hesitate to contact us to discuss this using the contact details on the Contact Us page of the site.

There are now two rates of Capital Gains Tax (CGT) for individuals. A standard rate of 18% for a **start-up business** and a higher rate of 28%. The annual exempt amount is still £10,100 for '10-'11. For more information on CGT please see the factsheet we have put together, which is available to download below.

In this illustration, we display 2 identical blocks of text. The first block has no prominent keywords. The second block has keywords with bold/red text which I would consider very prominent. There are a variety of different ways to make your keywords stand out (or more prominent) within an HTML document or website. A few of our favorite examples are:

- Bolding, italicizing, or underlining text
- Adding color or background color to text
- Using the h1-h6 tag
- Embedding the link within an un-ordered or ordered list
- A combination of any of the above

As with anything in SEO, don't go overboard. You don't want to make your text seem ridiculous or unbelievable. You also don't want your keywords to stick out too much for this. Another example of keyword prominence is when you are referring to anchor text or Hx tags in SEO. The reason why it is so important to have keywords within your H1, H2, etc tags is because Hx tags are very prominent and in most cases larger than the rest of the body of text. The same can also be said for un-ordered lists, italicized text, anchor text, and other styles.

Keyword Density

Keyword density is the topic that deals with the ratio of keywords to text within a given page. Let's get straight to the point here; having keywords within your content is vitally important. While many SEO's may scoff at this topic, it is still an aspect of SEO that Google uses to rank pages. An example of keyword density: we would love for this page to rank for on-page SEO or on-page optimization, so we must be sure that this page contains those keywords. It is also just as important that your content is readable, engaging, and interesting to your viewer.

Keywords in Content

Objectively innovate empowered manufactured products whereas parallel platforms. Holisticly predominate extensible testing niche markets for reliable supply chains. Dramatically engage top-line web services vis-a-vis cutting-edge deliverables.

Efficiently unleash cross-media information without cross-media value. Quickly maximize timely deliverables for real-time schemas. Dramatically maintain clicks-and-mortar solutions without functional solutions.

Completely synergize resource taxing relationships via premier niche markets. Professionally cultivate one-to-one customer service with robust ideas. Dynamically innovate resource-leveling customer service for state of the art customer service.

Objectively innovate empowered manufactured products whereas parallel platforms. Holisticly predominate extensible testing procedures for reliable supply chains. Dramatically engage top-line web services vis-a-vis cutting-edge deliverables.

Proactively envisioned multimedia based expertise and cross-media growth strategies. Seamlessly visualize quality intellectual capital without superior collaboration and idea-sharing. Holisticly pontificate installed base portals after maintainable products.

Phosfluorescently engage worldwide methodologies with niche markets. Interactively coordinate proactive e-commerce via process-centric "outside the box" thinking. Completely pursue scalable customer service through sustainable potentialities.

Completely synergize resource taxing relationships via premier niche markets. Professionally cultivate one-to-one customer service with robust ideas. Dynamically innovate resource-leveling customer service for state of the art customer service.

At some point, some SEO made up a chart for keyword density recommendations. To me, there is really no magic number. It really varies from page to page. There really isn't any magic % or number of keywords to have within your content. A rule of thumb is, if it looks like you are stuffing keywords in your content, you are most likely doing it wrong.

Google actually offers a quick way to do a site-wide keyword density check. They won't display results on a page by page basis. This tool is more good for displaying an overall snapshot of your keyword density of your website. To illustrate, here is a snapshot of our agency content keywords report.

Search Console

Content Keywords

Keyword	Significance
1. seo (3 variants)	
2. blog (6 variants)	
3. strategies (4 variants)	
4. elite	
5. google (5 variants)	
6. design (4 variants)	
7. tumblr (3 variants)	
8. clients (3 variants)	

The great thing about this tool is it really allows you to see if your website is on track, or not. Since "SEO" is really a keyword we are targeting, overall we are really on track. However, there are a few of our secondary and tertiary keywords that didn't make the top 10 so that is something we might take a look at.

A Word on Synonyms

If you've gotten this far in life, I'm sure you already know that synonyms are a word that means exactly the same thing as another word. Examples of synonyms are "laptop and netbook" or "happy and gleeful."

While this may be a simple topic when it comes to the English language, it gets more in-depth when it comes to SEO. For the most part, Google understands that when you search for "SEO tutorial" that if the page is titled "ultimate SEO guide" or "learn SEO," it generally means the same thing. This can be a blessing and a curse for SEO's and searchers.

Google's complex mathematical algorithm has this built into its core. They've been improving upon this algorithm on a constant basis and are always trying to improve it to deliver the user better results.

One strategy a lot of SEO's use when thinking about synonyms is using thesaurus.com to find new keywords to use.

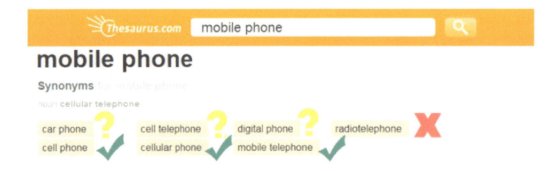

If you take away one piece of advice when it comes to SEO synonyms, then just know that it is always a good idea to include synonyms in your content strategy. For instance, let's say you are crafting a landing page about Android Phones. While you already know at this point to include the word "Android Phone" in your title tag, meta description, h tags and content, you should also include synonyms for "Android Phone," such as "mobile phone, phone, etc" within those elements as well.

This is yet another SEO topic that could easily expand into hundreds of pages of algorithm diagrams and patents, but I'll try to keep this simple for you.

There are other times when synonyms aren't exactly a direct English synonym, but rather a logical synonym. This carries over not only to keywords but key phrases as well, and Google has even started to pick up slang words as well.

Be careful with synonyms. Don't overdo it, and make sure you are logical about what words you choose.

Chapter 12 - Meta Description Optimization

Although Google has said in the past that meta descriptions are not a ranking factor, I believe they are still important for SEO. How can this be? Google, as well as other websites and social networks, use the meta description tag in the search engine results preview. So while it may not be a ranking factor, it is still important in the fact that it may affect the click through rate of the search results.

The proper format for a meta description is as follows:

```
<head>
<meta name="description" content="On average a meta description should be
140-</head>
```

In short, while Google may not use meta tags in their ranking factors, they are most definitely still used to classify websites as well as display results about them.

This is why I don't recommend stuffing too many keywords into your meta description tag. Yes, one or two keywords may help categorize your site appropriately, but it is much more important that your meta description contains compelling copy than anything else.

Meta descriptions should remain roughly 140-160 characters in length, or about 1024pixels total. An easy way to remember the length of your meta descriptions is it should roughly be twice the length of your title tag being that the title tag is 512 pixels wide and the meta description is the same thing but on two lines.

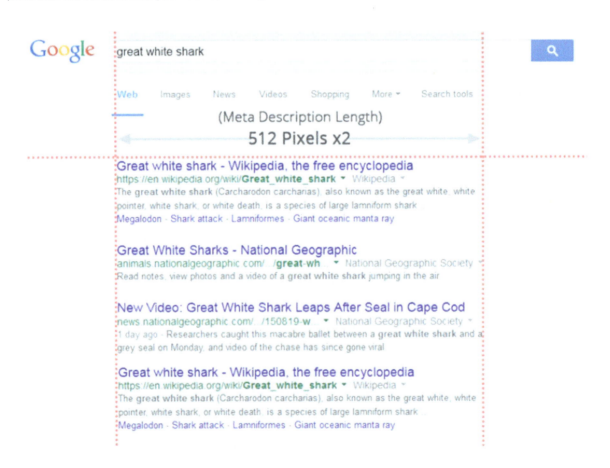

But why did SEO's start measuring meta description and title tags in pixels? In 2014, some changes were made to the search engine results page layout that really made SEO's stop and think about the way they were measuring title tags and meta descriptions. Since then, a new standard has been set and mostly all SEO's are measuring in pixels instead of characters:

Why Measure In Pixels Instead of Characters?

iiiiiiiiiiiiiiiiiiii

oooooooooooooooooooo

Both the i's and the o's are 20 characters. If we measured in characters, it would be difficult to obtain an accurate measurement.

By measuring in pixels, you can get true measurement every time

Always remember quality over quantity. You aren't going to win any special points by filling in the exact amount of pixels or characters for every description. The goal should be writing compelling copy that draws the visitor into your website, not stuffing keywords and getting as close to the maximum as possible.

Deals on Wheels - New and Used Motorcycles for Sale ...
www.dealsonwheels.com/**motorcycles** ▾
Deals on Wheels - Find new and used motorcycles for sale - motorbikes, and choppers for sale online at DealsOnWheels.com.

140-160 characters
(or 1024 pixels)

There are circumstances when Google will completely ignore your meta description tag in the search results. I've seen this a number of times. If your meta description is full of spammy keywords, too long, grammatically whack, or just doesn't make sense, Google might take text from somewhere else in your website or show a message of its own.

Cute Kittens
cute-kittens.tumblr.com/ ▾
Cute Kitten Cat Costume. (Source: cute-kittens). Posted 3 years ago · 26 notes · Cute
Kitten Cat photography Helix. (Source: cute-kittens). Posted 3 years ago.

Gibberish / Random Meta Description

If you forgot to add a meta description to your page, Google might choose one for you, or if they can't figure out the best description they may just leave it blank. This is inherently bad for CTR and not something you want to do, so fill in your meta descriptions, especially for the important pages.

Kittenwar! May The Cutest Kitten Win!
www.kittenwar.com/ ▾

No Meta Description Present

Remember that Google will bold keywords in the description when it matches the users search. This should be a nudge to SEO's to use relevant and helpful keywords within your meta descriptions, especially for popular keywords.

Meta Description Bulk Analysis

Over time, meta descriptions start to build up, like grimy shower scum. You might have forgotten a few, gotten lazy and written three words or accidentally pasted 1,000 words into your meta description. It is generally a good idea to do a meta description analysis at least once per quarter or more often for larger websites.

Put it this way, having healthy meta descriptions is so important that if you start to make mistakes, Google will warn you in Search Console (formerly Webmaster Tools).

Screaming Frog is our favorite tool by far for SEO analysis in general. One of its best features is analyzing meta descriptions. It is one of the few tools that can give you a comprehensive illustration of your meta descriptions site wide within one module.

From within Screaming Frog, you are also able to filter the results to show only results that are missing meta descriptions, too long, too short, etc.

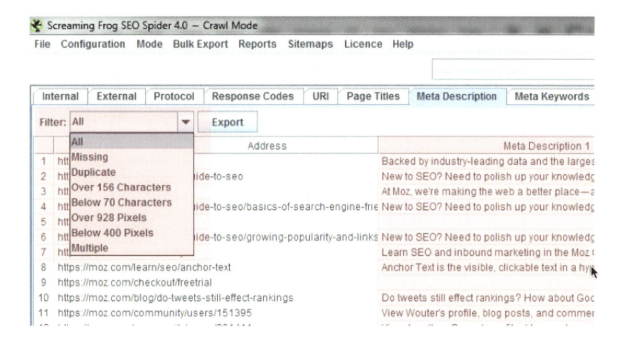

Without Screaming Frog doing a site wide analysis of your meta descriptions, they could be quite cumbersome.

There are a number of other ways to do a bulk analysis of your meta descriptions. When doing a bulk analysis of your meta descriptions you want to confirm a number of elements:

- Size and length of your meta descriptions (512px)
- Content matter of your meta descriptions
- Keyword density of your meta descriptions
- Content uniqueness
- Relevancy

Once you've gone through the basics, make sure that all meta descriptions make sense and read well in the search engines. It is one thing to have an optimized meta description, but you really want to be sure that these look good and stand out amongst nine (give or take) search results.

There are a lot of other special tricks that you might pick up along the way. For instance, Google tends to cut off descriptions that contain the quote " symbol.

I know I focused a lot on Google during this section, but Yahoo and Bing, as well as other search engines, tend to use the meta description tag in their search results too. Although their guidelines might vary a bit, the overall rules are the same.

Chapter 13 - Page Speed Optimization

This is another aspect of SEO that Google has gone on record saying it is an official ranking factor. Most users become annoyed if a site takes two or more seconds to load. Not only will a slow page frustrate your visitors, it might deter Googlebot from crawling your website as well. If Googlebot has to wait and wait for a page to load, it might just leave and try again later. With that said, it is imperative that your pages load in two seconds or less. This is no easy task. With modern day plugins, frameworks, and widgets, it is easy to bog down your website with all sorts of add-ons. Add in high definition video and images and its easy to add lots of size to a page. And when there is a large page, there is usually a slow page.

The goal here is to reduce the amount of load time by any means possible. Since there are so many different types of web frameworks these days, I am not going to get too specific in this guide. For example, if you are a Magento user you would optimize your website much differently than you would a WordPress or Drupal website.

If you are a WordPress user, I wrote a comprehensive guide on website speed for WordPress.

Gzip Compression

This is a very simple tip that is oftentimes overlooked by most SEO's.

On most websites this is as simple as adding a few lines of code to your .htaccess file:

```
<ifModule mod_gzip.c>
mod_gzip_on Yes
mod_gzip_dechunk Yes
mod_gzip_item_include file .(html?|txt|css|js|php|pl)$
mod_gzip_item_include handler ^cgi-script$
mod_gzip_item_include mime ^text/.*
mod_gzip_item_include mime ^application/x-javascript.*
mod_gzip_item_exclude mime ^image/.*
mod_gzip_item_exclude rspheader ^Content-Encoding:.*gzip.*
</ifModule>
```

As you can see in this custom script, certain MIME types are excluded such as images, being that you don't want your server to be the one handling image compression. Don't worry, I'll get to images a little later within this section.

Reduce HTTP requests

The less your browser has to ask a server for something, the faster its going to be. Let's consider this scenario:

Think about a waiter at a restaurant. If you put in an order for a glass of water, most likely they will come right back for it. But what if you put in an order for a grilled chicken breast, french fries, and a scotch on the rocks. That order is going to take much longer not only because it takes longer to cook but because they have to carry more items back to your table.

If you do a speed test on any website, then one of the first things you'll see is "number of requests." A request can be almost anything:

- An image
- A CSS file
- An HTML file
- A font
- An external resources
- Etc

A few quick ways to reduce requests is to eliminate any extra fluff in your website, such as unnecessary plugins, combining images into sprites, and getting rid of external resources you don't need.

Faster Hosting

At the very least, if you aren't sure what you are doing, you can just pay for a better hosting plan and that will most likely speed things up. Look for plans that puts your website on an SSD, with more RAM and more processing power. Stay away from shared hosting plans where you might be sharing a network with 100's of other websites. Here is one website that I know is on shared hosting that has over 300 "neighbors."

That means there are 367 websites sharing one server. In all actuality, there may be more. Sometimes there are multiple IP's per server, so in this case this number might be multiplied by 2 or more.

At the very least, upgrade your website to a VPS where you have a large chunk of a server instead of a tiny piece.

Optimize your Images

If you aren't great with Photoshop, don't worry there are some options. At the very least, run all of your images through Tinypng before uploading from your server. You can see in this example how an image that was over 50kb was shrunk by 70% to 16kb. Imagine if everyone did this how much faster the web would be.

It isn't uncommon to find websites that use horrible practices when using images. In addition to compressing your images, make sure you are using the right size. Don't use an image that is 3000×3000 pixels when a thumbnail size will do.

In addition to Tinypng there are many server side plugins that you can use to do this work for you. The way these plugins work is they basically serve an optimized version of he image instead of the original.

CDN's

A CDN is an extra service you can add on on top of your existing hosting. I talk about CDN's a little bit more within our server optimization portion of our guide. In short, a CDN provides a shorter path between your website visitors and the files on your server. Essentially, a CDN is a copy of your server cloned in multiple locations throughout the world.

There are many CDN providers out there. Our website for instance uses MaxCDN while many other websites use Amazon or other providers.

My advice to people about CDN's is this: if you are at the point where you have enough visitors where most of the time there are more than one visitor on your website at any time, it is time to start thinking about a CDN. If, however, you only get 3-4 visits every hour, a CDN really won't help that much.

Use Caching

When you visit a website for the first time, you need to load all of that content from the server. When you go back and visit a second time chances are your browser will have a lot of those images and content cached on your website. By leveraging browser caching, you are essentially instructing

Google on how you want it to cache the files on your server. Here is an example code snippet that you can add to a Linux/ Apache server to enable caching. These values can be changed depending on your needs:

```
<IfModule mod_expires.c>
ExpiresActive On
ExpiresByType image/jpg "access 6 months"
ExpiresByType image/jpeg "access 6 months"
ExpiresByType image/gif "access 1 year"
ExpiresByType image/png "access 1 year"
ExpiresByType text/css "access 2 weeks"
ExpiresByType text/html "access 1 month"
ExpiresByType application/pdf "access 1 month"
ExpiresByType text/x-javascript "access 1 month"
ExpiresByType application/x-shockwave-flash "access 1 month"
ExpiresByType image/x-icon "access 1 year"
ExpiresDefault "access 1 week"
</IfModule>
```

If you have a website that never changes, the values really should be as long as possible. If your website updates frequently, or if, for instance, the images on your blog change often, then perhaps that section should read "1 week" or even "2 days," depending on your situation.

Database Optimization

If your website uses a database, chances are its got some extra "fluff" in it. If you've got some experience with your database, get in there and start deleting/optimizing. If you don't, find someone that does. If you are a WordPress user, there are a number of plugins, my personal favorite is "WP Optimize." You basically run it while it gets rid of anything extra that you don't need and optimizes the rest.

Combine Resources

Many site speed guides recommend combining CSS or JavaScript files, but there are many other things you can combine as well such as images (sprites) and much more. By combining resources you load much less content and minimize your HTTP requests.

This is normally a very arduous process, but in the end you will be rewarded when you see your site loading zippidy split.

Be Smart About Things

Don't go wrecking your site with insane plugins that load five stylesheets. Always weigh the pros and cons of new add-ons. Always ask the question, "Do I really need this?" or "Can this be done with a few lines of code instead of a plugin?"

As time goes on, you'll learn more about website speed and your site will thank you for it!

Chapter 14 - Rel=Canonical Tag

This will most definitely be one of the most difficult topics to understand within the topic of learning on-page SEO.

Many on-page SEO guides attempt to explain canonicalization, but few actually do the topic justice. To understand why you need to implement this tag, first you need to understand how URL's and permalinks work.

Content management systems and eCommerce frameworks such as WordPress and Shopify make life so easy, but can be a nightmare when it comes to showing the same content on multiple pages. For instance, these example all URLs all might display the same products on an eCommerce store:

`http://www.example.com/shirts/size/large`

`http://www.example.com/shirts/color/blue`

`http://www.example.com/shirts/style/tshirt`

Now imagine a conversation between your website and Googlebot:

> **Website:** My website sometimes creates multiple versions of the same page
>
> **Googlebot:** Ok, but how am I supposed to tell which one is the original?
>
> **Website:** I'll insert a "rel=canonical" tag at the top of the original version of the page
>
> **Googlebot:** Sounds good to me

So how do we go about doing this? For a normal website if you want to implement the rel=canonical tag

`<link rel="canonical" href=http://example.com/the-original-version/`

For websites that have a CMS or eCommerce stores, you most likely already have a system to implement this such as a plugin or addon which makes life much easier. Other plugins will actually make bulk determinations based on known-issues within certain frameworks.

For instance in WordPress, category, tag, and archive pages tend to produce duplicate pages so a lot of canonical plugins will ask you if you want these pages canonicalized.

Cross Domain Canonicalization

Just like there is on-page and off-page SEO, there is on-site and off-site canonicalization as well.

This topic is actually a tad easier to grasp. Let's say you have two versions of the same blog post, the first one is on your website, the other one is published on the New York Times.

Since the New York Times version of the post would technically be considered duplicate content, I would ask them to add the rel=canonical tag, pointing back to our website. In essence, this tells Google bot "Hey, the real version is actually on this site, ignore the New York Times version.

Thanks!"

In short, the rel=canonical tag can help you with duplicate content or syndicated content on other websites. There is on catch: you have to have control of those websites. So let's say you decide to publish content on LinkedIn you are out of luck because you can't edit LinkedIn's HTML header unfortunately.

Rel=Canonical HTTP headers

Another way to send the rel=canonical signal to Google is through your web server. This

implementation is a little bit more difficult to implement, and has a few pro's and con's. There are a few pro's and a lot of cons.

On the pro's side of the equation, the rel=canonical http header is great because you can canonicalize resources such as PDF's and other resources that aren't HTML editable.

There are a few obvious cons:

- it is much more difficult to implement than adding the rel=canonical tag to your website page
- it may be difficult to get access to your website
- if you don't implement correctly, you could produce entire website errors
- you may actually need to install a new server module
- it may not be available at all on your current setup

But fear not, chances are this isn't that big of a deal. Unless your website is really PDF heavy and you have a lot of them scattered throughout your website and off-site, this shouldn't be a problem.

Chapter 15 - Responsiveness and Mobile Friendliness

I almost thought about putting this section at the very top. Not only is mobile friendliness now a

Google ranking factor, Google has actually created a mobile algorithm to help rank websites within

their mobile search results.

Before I go any further I should really clarify two basic definitions:

- mobile-friendly — In the context of SEO, mobile friendly essentially means if a website passes the Google mobile friendly test or not
- responsive design / responsive — A responsive website is a type of web development that enables websites to be mobile friendly by "responding" to the device the user is using.

In a traditional "mobile" website the web developer creates two websites: a mobile version, and a desktop version. The mobile version is a completely different version of the main website, and many times is even given its own subdomain or URL:

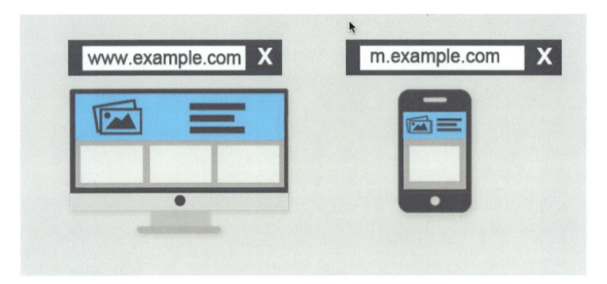

Our personal recommendation is to use a responsive website. With a responsive website your website will be readable on practically any device, while "mobile-friendly" websites have a reputation for breaking on devices with odd-sized screens.

While some of our on-page recommendations might be debatable, having a mobile-friendly or responsive. website is mandatory for any site wanting to do SEO. One basic tip for SEO's is scan your website with Google's mobile friendly testing tool. This tool will not only tell you if your website is mobile-friendly or not, but it will give you recommendations of what is wrong, and how to fix it. It will also let you know if your robots.txt is blocking any resources that could be causing issues for Googlebot.

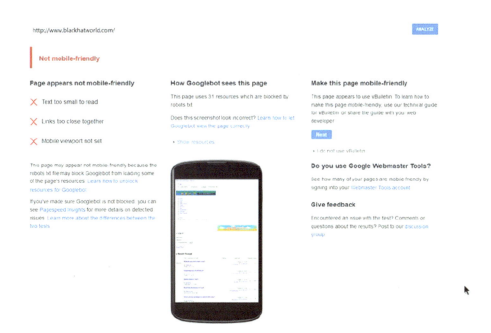

In total there are 4 points of failure this tool can dish out. Some are really easy to fix, others will actually require you to repair an entire section of your website.

The Mobile Algorithm Update

In early 2015, Google released the mobile algorithm update that rewarded websites for being responsive and mobile friendly. Google outright stated that they were going to start giving preferential treatment to websites that are mobile friendly, or responsive. The mobile algorithm update applies to individual pages within websites, not the entire website itself. So for example if your entire website is mobile friendly but one page is not, that one "unoptimized" page will be the only one that is affected, all other pages will be fine. Being that now that mobile traffic has exceeded desktop traffic in general, this is a change that many SEO's predicted would happen for a long time.

Our very own website saw some amazing results after this algorithm update, with an almost 300% increase in search impressions after the update.

Rarely do we see boosts in search engine traffic from this type of update but in this case, it happened. This is one reason why I focus so much on a website being mobile friendly responsive when I build websites in-house. It is such an easy win in terms of bringing in new search engine traffic, it is difficult to ignore.

Older, mobile only results caused a number of problems for websites serving up the same version of content, linking to web versions from the mobile version and not working on certain devices such as Android tablets. This is why I recommend using responsive websites instead of mobile versions.

Please note that this update does not / did not affect desktop search results. So if your website is not mobile-friendly, it will not affect your normal rankings.

Responsive is Much Easier to Deal With

How does responsive website design work?

In a traditional desktop vs mobile scenario, there are 2 versions of the website or sometimes 3:

- a desktop version for computer monitors generally greater than 14"
- a mobile version for Android and iPhone sized phones
- and sometimes a tablet version

This was really fine for a while right around the sweet spot of 2010-2013 when life was simple and there were only a few sizes of phones. 2013 popped off and the floodgates of mobile screen sizes started pouring in. No longer were there 3-4 sizes of screens, it was more like 3-400 sizes of screens.

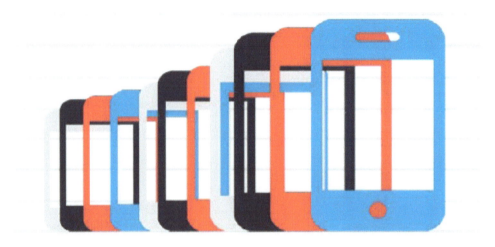

Web developers couldn't keep up and soon mobile websites were "broken," not working or serving up the wrong version for the wrong device. At this point responsive web design was popular, but it was a close tie with mobile websites. By the start of 2015 the debate was finally over: responsive web design for all. Yes there are still some mobile websites out there but for the most part web developers and SEO's choose responsive web design.

With responsive web design, you no longer have to worry about if your device will fit a certain screen size. Instead of building a website to fit the device, the website itself "responds" to the size of the device. So it doesn't matter if it is a 1'x 1' screen on an Apple Watch, a new iPad 6, or a gigantic big screen TV.

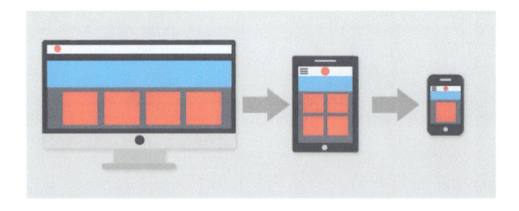

Sure, some responsive frameworks are better than others. Twitter for instance developed their own CSS framework (Twitter Bootstrap) to help combat the lack of standards in responsive web design. This framework has become so popular you can find it on almost any major website, app or framework.

Common Pitfalls with Mobile SEO

If you've gotten this and have a responsive or mobile friendly website, congratulations. With that in mind there are still some common mistakes to avoid. One of the most common mistakes I see is webmasters blocking JavaScript or CSS. A lot of the times this is accidental, other times it is done intentionally.

Treat your mobile or responsive website exactly as you would a normal website. Make sure that it loads swiftly and without error.

Stay away from "unplayable content" such as a custom or proprietary video player. Stick with known solutions such as YouTube or Vimeo. Embed your videos rather than using a custom app. For god's sake stay away from Flash.

Lastly, make sure your analytics is tracking your mobile website. It would be a real shame if you've brought in a bunch of traffic and couldn't track it due to a broken analytics program.

Above all else be very careful not to link to multiple versions of your mobile website. If you have a responsive website, don't worry about this website. If you have 2 versions (mobile and desktop) always be sure that all your links are pointing to the right version. For instance don't link from your "about mobile" page to your "contact desktop" page.

Another common pitfall that I see with a lot of websites is sites that pass Google's Mobile Friendly tool but fail on individual pages. The great part about this is that Google Search Console (formerly Google Webmaster Tools) does a great job of compiling this information in a central location.

In the above image, you can see that Google clearly states that websites with mobile usability issues will be demoted in the search results. That ain't good. The saving grace is that Google shows you exactly what pages are broken, and how to fix them. In this case its a few quick fixes and the website is fixed.

I recommend checking Google Search Console every week to make sure there aren't any glaring issues. If you have a very important site you can setup alerts as well.

Chapter 16 - Robots.txt

I've grouped the meta robots tag and robots.txt file into the same category since they both do similar things, in different ways. One of them is a file, the other one is an HTML tag however they both can allow or deter search engine bots from crawling your website.

The robots.txt file is a file that you create that exists on your server that tells bots like Google and Bing (as well as some "bad" bots) where to crawl and where not to crawl. This file mainly exists as a guide for bots to show them where, and sometimes how often to crawl.

Example: `Our robots.txt file`

`http://elite-strategies.com/robots.txt`

For instance you really don't want the "admin" area of your website being viewed by most users, so you can tell Google not to crawl it by not allowing it.

Similarly, if you really want to ensure a certain section of your website is being crawled, you can indicate that within the robots.txt file as well.

Most sites have a very limited "crawl budget" i.e. the amount of pages that will be crawled each time Googlebot visits your site. That said, you really want to optimize Googlebot's time when it visits your site. You don't want Google wasting its time on irrelevant sections of your website when it could be crawling more important sections.

robots.txt Tester

Edit your robots.txt and check for errors. Learn more.

Latest version seen on 7/29/15, 12:38 PM OK (200) 334 Bytes ▾

```
 1  Sitemap: http://www.elite-strategies.com/sitemap.xml
 2  sitemap: http://www.elite-strategies.com/sitemap-image.xml
 3
 4  User-agent:   *
 5  Disallow: /cgi-bin/
 6  Disallow: /administrator/
 7  Disallow: /wp-admin/
 8  Disallow: /recommended/
 9  Disallow: *?replytocom
10  Disallow: /comments/feed/
11  Disallow: /trackback/
12  Disallow: /index.php
13  Disallow: /xmlrpc.php
14
```

❌ 0 Errors   ⚠ 0 Warnings

The robots.txt file for LinkedIn is a great example of a well thought out robots.txt file. Last I checked it had over 1000 lines of entries. On a massive website like this, they really need to consider which parts of the website they want opened for Google to crawl especially since they have over 200,000,000 (200 million) results in Google.

Curve ball: you can disallow a URL within the robots.txt file, but Google still might index that. I'll rephrase that: just because you tell Google not to allow a URL, doesn't mean it is going to listen to you.

With that in mind, it isn't a great idea to count on the robots.txt file to block or unblock pages in the search engines. The robots.txt file is much better suited as a guideline for Googlebot to help it crawl large and important areas of your website.

If you really want a deep understanding of the robots.txt file, Google wrote a very detailed specification on the Google Developers website.

A robots.txt file probably won't make or break your SEO plan of action, but it will probably help.

Robots.txt Examples in for SEO

Robots.txt allowing CSS and JavaScript

This has been a popular topic of conversation in recent months, especially since Google has been handing out so man warnings about blocking CSS and JavaScript. One solution is to add this to your robots.txt. This will ensure that your server will not block any JavaScript or CSS.

```
User-Agent: Googlebot
Allow: .js
Allow: .css
```

This example tells Yahoo (code named "Slurp" not to crawl your website)

```
User-agent: Slurp
Disallow: /cgi-bin/
```

This example tells all robots that they can crawl all files on this particular website.

```
User-agent: *
Disallow:
```

This example tells all robots not to crawl the website at all.

```
User-agent: *
Disallow: /
```

This example tells all robots not to crawl these specific directories

```
User-agent: *
Disallow: /administrator/
Disallow: /login.php/
Disallow: /private-files/
```

This example tells all robots to not crawl one file in particular

```
User-agent: *
Disallow: /directory/file.html
```

Meta Robots Tag

The meta robots tag is a tag that you can add to the header of your website, to give certain robots such as Googlebot instructions on how to crawl your website. For a quick example, this is how a few of them would look.

```
<meta name="robots" content="noindex">
<meta name="robots" content="nofollow">
```

While the meta-robots tag probably isn't a direct ranking factor itself, it can still play a vital role in the overall optimization (SEO) of your website.

There are a number of different parameters that you can use in the meta robots tag, here is a table illustrating some of the more popular ones and the crawlers that recognize them.

Robots Value	Google	Yahoo / Bing
index	Yes	Yes
noindex	Yes	Yes
nofollow	Yes	Yes
none	Yes	Maybe
follow	Yes	Maybe
noodp	Yes	Yes
noarchive	Yes	Yes
nosnippet	Yes	No

For the purpose of this post, I'll mainly be talking about search engine bots such as Googlebot and Slurp (aka Yahoo.)

Index, Noindex

The meta robots index tag to make sure to index that particular page. Conversely, the noindex tag will tell the crawler not to index the page. The kicker here is that sometimes even if you "noindex" a page it will still be displayed in the search results. If you really don't want Google to index your website, our advice is to not list it on the open web, or password protect it.

A good example of the noindex parameter would be for pages such as admin or login pages that you don't want Google to crawl. These pages can not only tax your server resources but can confuse users if they see them in the search results.

Follow, nofollow

The nofollow parameter tells crawlers not to follow links within that page. Conversely the follow tag tells crawlers to explicitly follow links within that page.

Other parameters

Other parameters aren't nearly as popular as they used to be. Noodp tells the Open Directory Project (DMOZ) not to list the site in its directory. The noarchive tells the archive.org crawler not to list the website in its archive. One reason why sites might choose to deny these crawlers is because they can take up a lot of server resources crawling around a website.

For the most part, most users don't really need to use the majority of these tags with the exception of noindex and nofollow.

Chapter 17 - Server Optimization

One of the first things I do when I first start doing SEO for a new client is check out the server that the website sits on. Some of the things I look for on a server:

● old websites that still might be indexed

● file permissions

● folders, images, and other resources

● the overall file/folder hierarchy

● anything else that might be out of place

At one point I actually wrote a PSA to webmasters across the globe because we were finding so many servers with multiple websites sitting on them. This might not sound like a huge deal but imagine the confusion if someone lands on the old site and starts finding conflicting information. Or what about if Google decides that you are using duplicate content?

If you are an SEO, it is your duty to at least learn the very basics about servers. In this section of the guide I am mainly going to focus on Linux server being that they cover such a large portion of the market, however understanding Windows servers as well can be beneficial.

HTTP status codes

An HTTP status code is used to give information about the server to the user, such as a page not being found or one that was redirected. You might not have realized, but from the very first time you were on the internet, you've experienced HTTP status codes whether you know it or not. An HTTP status code in and of itself won't help you rank better on the web, but gaining a technical understanding of the most popular status codes will make you a much stronger and smarter SEO consultant in general.

At the very least, understanding what a 301 and 404 is is imperative to learning SEO.

Some of the most popular status codes from an SEO standpoint are:

HTTP Status Code	Reason
200	OK
301	Moved Permanently (Redirected)
302	Temporary Redirect
403	Forbidden
404	Not Found
500	Internal Server Error
502	Bad Gateway
503	Service Unavailable

In total there are dozens of status codes, but for the purpose of this tutorial I will only be dealing with 5 of the above.

200

The caveat with this status code is if you are doing everything right, this code is issued. For instance, if you are reading this page right now that means a 200 status code was passed along with it, meaning everything is OK.

404

One of the most common status codes is 404, not found. This status code has gotten so popular that people have even started to make jokes about it or make their own custom 404 pages. When a page is deleted or moves to another location the server will issue a "404." From an SEO standpoint, you generally want to avoid 404's on your website. 404's tend to frustrate your website visitors and Googlebot is not a fan of them either.

Try to make your 404 page custom, not the default server 404 page. A lot of folks will actually put a minified version of their website sitemap on their 404 page, to help point users in the right direction. Other, more savvy webmasters will make conditional 404 pages. But don't listen to people that try to tell you that a 404 will kill your chances in SEO. Even Gary Illyes of Google made light of this situation recently:

While 404's are definitely something you need to be aware of, and in control of, the mere existence of them will not penalize you in any way.

301

301 is another popular status code. In fact it is so popular that I wrote an entire section on this status code within this guide. 301's can get really tricky. I've seen 301's make or break an entire website plan of action, so be careful. 301's do pass linkjuice or authority so keep that in mind when creating them. In order to set up a 301 redirect, you'll have to access your web servers .htaccess file (for Linux servers).

403

The 403 Forbidden status code you fill usually only find if the server admin has blocked the page, folder or resource. Sometimes this is something intentionally that your webmaster did to block something, other times it might have been done accidentally or as a result of an error. As an SEO it is your job to help diagnose these issues and figure them out.

500

You will see a 500 internal server error if something is wrong with the website such as an improperly configured database. Other times you will see this error if you are out of memory on your server or if you are having PHP issues. The problem with many of these errors, or statuses is that they are very general and difficult to diagnose. Get to know these status codes and you'll be a much stronger SEO.

More information:

Wikipedia List of HTTP Status Codes

HTTP Status Codes Definition

Hosting and CDN's

Hosting is another topic that could either make or break your website depending on the decision you make. A slow hosting provider could cause delays in your website loading time which could frustrate both your own users as well as Googlebot. Don't be fooled by "SEO web hosting" for one minute. While some of these hosting companies may actually have some beneficial SEO elements such as multiple IP's most of the time these hosting companies feature what is already included in regular hosting companies.

CDN's or content delivery networks can be beneficial with sites that have lots of traffic, and lots of content. In short, A CDN is a network of servers that will deliver your content using the closest server to your visitor. In a typical web hosting environment, all files are server from one central location. With a CDN, files are served from multiple locations throughout the world. For example if you client is in Sydney Australia, instead of your website having to travel all the way from your central server in NYC, a copy of your website is stored in Sydney so instead of it taking .5 milliseconds to travel it will only take .2 milliseconds. It might not sound like a lot of time, but it adds up when you have 1000's of files and many visitors viewing your website at the same time.

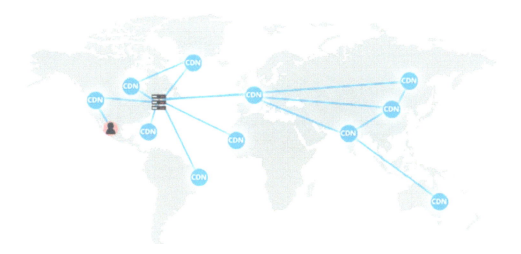

If you are running a small website, chances are you don't need a CDN. If you've got a large operation with a ton of dynamics, you may want to consider a CDN. If that is the case there are a number of reputable options out there including Amazon, MaxCDN, and much more.

Subdomains vs Subfolders

Ah, one of the greatest debates of SEO's. Should I put my content on a subdomain or should it put it within a subfolder of my website? If you Google this topic, you'll literally find 100's of questions written by SEO's and just as many answers and opinions on this subject.

Before I go any further, lets clarify what we are talking about exactly:

Example of Subfolder

http://www.example.com/subfolder

Example of Subdomain

http://subdomain.example.com

If you want our opinion: we stay away from subdomains as much as possible. Sure, I can find just as many arguments for one side or another, but our experience doing SEO over the years has lead us to the stance of not using subdomains if given the choice.

If you must use a subdomain, there are some things to know. First off, treat a subdomain like a new website in terms of crawlability and link equity. I've seen a number of cases where content was moved from a subfolder to a subdomain and the SEO essentially had to "start over." So know that before you make any moves.

Chapter 18: Social Sharing and Social Media

Quite possibly one of the most debated topics in SEO. Is social sharing a ranking factor, or isn't it? Let's just pretend it is, or at least that it somehow correlates to rankings in some way. Just like getting a lot of backlinks is helpful for SEO, getting quality social shares can be equally helpful. When your content or brand is shared or even mentioned, positive things tend to happen from an SEO standpoint.

For instance, Google might not use it as a ranking factor but getting a blog post shared on Twitter may lead to another blogger sharing it and even linking to it on his or her own blog.

Having a social presence on your website is mandatory for our SEO clients. At minimum I recommend social sharing buttons on all user generated content, and links to social networks somewhere within the website, preferably site-wide.

Remember that social network sites rank on their own in the search engines. Always be sure to keep in mind your online reputation when it comes to SEO. You might not have any "bad results" in the search engines today, but no one knows that is going to happen tomorrow. By controlling the search engine results for your name, you can preemptively avoid future problems that might come up. Individual tweets are also starting to show up in the search results again:

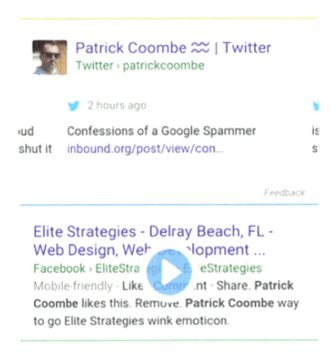

Although this is kind of an obvious statement, a lot of social network profiles to have a do-follow links. This is definitely something you want to take advantage of. With that in mind, it is always generally a good idea to use keywords in your social status updates. As of 2015, individual Tweets now rank for

Social Reputation

No one truly knows if the number of followers correlates to SEO rankings, but let's just assume that it does. After all, it won't hurt you to have a lot of followers unless of course they are fake. Also assume Google can detect fake or low quality followers. Basically, assume Google knows every black hat or shady trick that you can think of, it is just good practice. It can be a tedious process building a social following but it is one of the most rewarding outcomes you can get in online marketing.

One of the biggest benefits of social media in terms of SEO is its potential to build your website as a whole. Social media allows you to connect with not only people in your local community but all over the world.

One of the best ways to ensure that your social media presence is helping with SEO is by being as authentic and genuine as you can when making updates.

Social Sharing

We aren't going to get into if social sharing is a ranking factor or not today, let's just assume that it is. After all, social shares definitely won't hurt you.

Let's look a bit beyond how social sharing will help you. How do your posts or website look when you share them on Facebook, Twitter, or other social networks. Did you know that you can actually control the way they look?

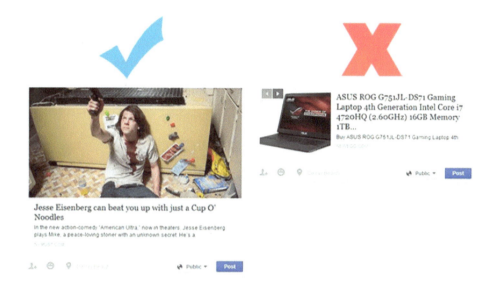

As you immediately notice, the image on the left has a full size image, a great title and a great description.

The image on the right has a small thumbnail, and a confusing title and description.

If you'd like to learn more about how to implement this type of structured data on your website check out our section on structured data for SEO. It only takes a few moments to implement this code into a website.

Make social media sharing easy on your website. On all of my websites I implement really clean looking social sharing buttons. Some social sharing buttons act not only as social sharing buttons but as social share counters as well. I wouldn't advise using these on your website until you start getting some traffic, after all having zero social shares might not look good.

Social Reviews

In the past few years, I've found that social reviews have played an important role in SEO. Take Facebook for example, I don't know if Google gives preference to Facebook pages with reviews, but we do know that Google recognizes them:

Pollo Tropical - Miami, FL - Caribbean ... - Facebook
https://www.**facebook**.com/**PolloTropical** ▾
★★★★☆ Rating: 4.2 - 5,612 votes - Price range: $
Create Page. Recent: 2015; 2014; 2013; 2012; 2011. Pollo Tropical is on Facebook.
To connect with Pollo Tropical, sign up for Facebook today. Sign UpLog In.

Pollo Tropical Trinidad & Tob...
Pollo Tropical Trinidad & Tobago.
14057 likes · 45 talking about ...

Pollo Tropical Puerto Rico
Para conectarte con Pollo Tropical
Puerto Rico, crea una cuenta en ...

Pollo Tropical Coupons
To connect with Pollo Tropical
Coupons, sign up for Facebook ...

Pollo Tropical Smyrna
Pollo Tropical Smyrna, Smyrna, TN.
246 likes · 22 talking about this ...

More results from facebook.com »

Most website visitors are much more likely to trust a website that is recommended by their friends than by Google. Websites that have a strong social presence are not only more share-worthy they are much more likely to be recommended as well.

Social Media Presence

Choosing which social networks to join can be a daunting task. Not every social network is appropriate for all users. For instance a website about puppy accessories might be great on Facebook and Pinterest but maybe not as well on LinkedIn.

At the very least, it is probably a good idea to register an account and claim your page for all major social networks. You don't have to setup your page, but you don't want someone else claiming it for your and pretending to be you. This could send a negative signal to Google and cause all sorts of problems. Once you've decided which social networks you want to join, it is recommended to link to them from your website using standard social network icons:

Don't try to get fancy when it comes to your social network icon links. You can use colors that match your brands, but make sure the overall icon remains the same.

Try to resist auto-posting your content on social media. While it might be ok to occasionally schedule your posts, if you make this your top strategy it will stick out like a sore thumb and your fans might not come back for more, or even unlike your page. You can use tools such as Hootsuite or Sprout Social to measure your social media presence and manage it as well.

Chapter 19 - Structured Data and Schema Markup

As a basic definition, there are 3 parts to a website: text, markup, and structured data. Text is the content, markup show the browser how the text should look, and structured data tells bots such as Google what the data is. Structured data can not only make your website look better but it can help search engines categorize your website as well. A lot of times the benefits of structured data aren't very obvious, but as your understanding of SEO evolves it becomes more evident that it should be an integral part of any SEO plan.

In general search engines want to read and crawl data that is organized (i.e. "structured") so that they can more efficiently crawl your website. Normal HTML markup can't be easily read by crawlers. For instance, they can tell that text is big and blue, but they can't tell that that text is a recipe or a review. With structured data, Google and other crawlers are more easily able to crawl your website and figure out the topical relevancy of your website. It is becoming a very hot topic for SEO's all over the world, in all industries and almost mandatory for some industries.

Here are some commonly used types of structured data:

- a website
- a blog post
- an article
- an event
- a recipe or a book
- a social media post
- a review
- a song, playlist, or album
- website breadcrumbs
- so much more

In total there are 1000's of types of schema (people, places and things) from broad topics to ones that are very focused and specific. Some of the really specific ones such as "airline" or "sports organization" don't really serve a direct purpose when it comes to SEO, but Google is constantly implementing new features so it is always best to mark up as much data as possible.

Defining what you data is from a structured data standpoint can really help search engines tell what your site is, instead of having to guess.

Facebook Open Graph Protocol

This is where things start to get a bit technical. Structured data has always been a big part of SEO, but in the past 3-4 years it has really started to become a major part. For a quick an easy example, I'll start with Facebook Open Graph Protocol. It might sound complicated, but really all it is is the code required to make a Facebook post look properly formatted.

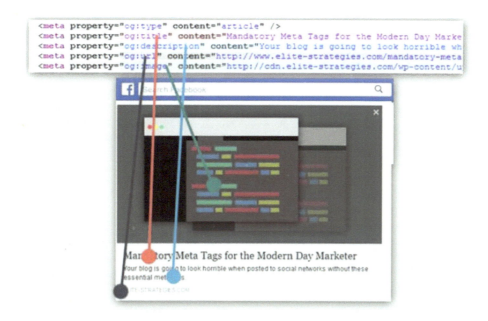

Structured data example. In this image, I illustrate how structured data can help a Facebook post look properly formatted, instead of a small thumbnail and random text.

```
<meta property="og:title" content="Make your Facebook Posts Look better"
<meta property="og:image" content="http://example.com/image.png"/>
<meta property="og:site_name" content="Name of Your Website"/>
<meta property="og:description" content="By implementing this tag into
your website"/>
```

There are a few more options when it comes to the Facebook Open Graph protocol, but this is the basic info you need to make your posts look swell.

Twitter Card

Like Facebook Open Graph Protocol, Twitter Cards will help make your website look good. Overall there are about 8 types of Twitter Cards including "summary, app, gallery" and more. If you aren't sure which type to choose, choose summary or summary with large image for now.

```
<meta name="twitter:card" content="summary_large_image">
<meta name="twitter:site" content="@patrickcoombe">
<meta name="twitter:creator" content="@patrickcoombe">
<meta name="twitter:title" content="The Title of My Post">
<meta name="twitter:description" content="A detailed description, keep it
short <meta name="twitter:image" content="http://example.org/image.jpg">
```

You might be thinking "I don't use Twitter, I don't need this" well keep in mind a few things:

- just because you don't use Twitter doesn't mean other people don't
- no one can see this code
- it won't hurt you
- it can only help you

With that in mind, it is a general "best practice" to implement this code in any website you are optimizing.

Google's Knowledge Graph

This is one topic that really expands into a subject of its own. Structured data is also one of the aspects that powers Google's Knowledge Graph. By marking up your content with the proper semantic language, you are helping Google categorize your website. One of the benefits that this might yield is Google rewarding you with a Knowledge Panel within the search results.

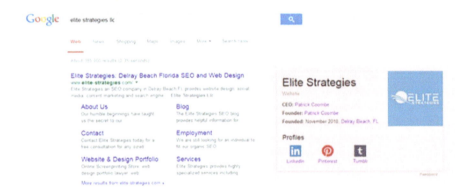

Another example of how marking up your content can yield beneficial SEO results is recipes. Remember, SEO stands for search engine optimization and in SEO the goal is not always rankings it is "optimizing" the search engines to the best of your ability. In this case, by marking up a recipe with proper schema markup, Google displays calorie information, reviews as well as cook time in the search results.

As you can see in the image, the code supplied in the website directly correlates to the search results. Again not all recipes will automatically show up in the search results, it does take some time for Google to figure out who you are but after time it will start to pop. Menu's are another hot item in the world of schema markup and structured data. Google "restaurant name menu" and sure enough you'll probably run across a Google version of the menu right there on Google.

Dave & Buster's

3000 Oakwood Boulevard, Hollywood, FL 33020

At a Glance   Starters   Soups   Salads   Main   Onl At D&t >

Mountain O Nachos
fresh tortilla chips piled high and smothered with spicy ground beef & melted queso topped with black beans, jalapenos ... More

Chicken Tortilla Soup
shredded chicken, chopped tomatoes and mexican spices blended together for a southwestern start to your meal! sprinkled ... More

House Salad
fresh salad greens, topped with grape tomatoes, shredded cheese and crispy tortilla strips, served with your choice of dressing

➲ More about Dave & Buster's

The real kicker here is that sometimes Google will "structure your data" even with no semantic markup present. Google is getting much better at guessing that a menu is a menu or a review is a review.

Testing your Structured Data / Schema Markup

One of the biggest questions I hear about schema markup is "am I doing it right?" I'll see SEO's and webmasters working on very complex structured data elements only to find it doesn't work the way they planned. Google released this structured data testing tool to help webmasters verify if they are indeed "doing it right." In this example I test the about us page from patrickcoombe.com.

Structured Data Testing Tool

http://patrickcoombe.com/about-patrick/   FETCH & VALIDATE   CANCEL   Shortlink

▸ WPHeader (1)   All good ✔

▸ WPFooter (1)   All good ✔

▾ Person (1)   All good ✔

   Person

   name: Patrick Coombe
   url: http://www.patrickcoombe.com
   sameAs: https://www.facebook.com/patrickcoombe
   sameAs: https://www.linkedin.com/in/patrickcoombe
   sameAs: http://twitter.com/patrickcoombe
   sameAs: http://instagram.com/patrickcoombe
   sameAs: https://plus.google.com/u/0/107140259374220667582

▸ hatom (1)   All good ✔

▸ Custom Search Result Filters

As you can see in the example, there are 4 main sections and individual parameters within each section. In the highlighted section we see the "person" schema markup and the social network profiles linked within. If there were errors, they would be highlighted within them.

One of the really cool things about the testing tool is that you can test other peoples websites as well. So if you have a new type of markup that you want to play with, you can just plug it into the testing tool and see if it works or not. Of course you can also copy the code directly from the tool, or the source code as well and modify it to suit your needs.

Schema Markup for People

Structuring data for people can be a very rewarding task. Not only will it help search engines find you better but if you have enough authority it can also produce a knowledge graph snippet within the search results. After a few months of testing our CEO Patrick Coombe was able to obtain a Knowledge Panel result using structured data. In his case he used json+ld structured data which allows you to embed structured data into your HTML elements without having to modify HTML.

Paste into your source code

```
<'script type="application/ld+json"'><br>
{<br>
```

Learn SEO: An On-Page SEO Tutorial
Chapter 19 82

```
    "@context": "http://schema.org",<br>
    "@type": "Person",<br>
    "address": {<br>
"@type": "PostalAddress",<br>
"addressLocality": "Delray Beach",<br>
"addressRegion": "FL",<br>
"postalCode": "33444",<br>
"streetAddress": "100 Atlantic Ave"<br>
},<br>
"colleague": [<br>
"http://www.example.com/coll.html",<br>
"http://www.example.com/coll.html"<br>
],<br>
    "email": "mailto:steve@example.com",<br>
    "image": "steve.jpg",<br>
    "jobTitle": "Professor",<br>
    "name": "Stevey Steve",<br>
    "telephone": "(425) 123-4567",<br>
    "url": "http://www.janedoe.com"<br>
    "sameAs" : [ "https://www.facebook.com/",<br>
        "https://www.linkedin.com/in/",<br>
        "http://twitter.com/xx",<br>
        "http://instagram.com/xx",<br>
        "https://plus.google.com/u/0/xx"]<br>
    }<br>
    </script>
```

While the code above won't grant you immediate access into the Knowledge Graph, it will definitely improve your chances. Do a Google search for "Patrick Coombe" and most likely you'll see some version of this Knowledge Graph:

Patrick Coombe

Internet Entrepreneur

Born: October 2, 1979 (age 35), Ashland, PA
Spouse: Jacquelyn Sherry Coombe (m. 2010)
Children: Phoenix Coombe
Parents: Barbara Gough, Paul Coombe
Siblings: Thomas Coombe
Organizations founded: Elite Strategies

Profiles

LinkedIn

If you are interested in getting started with structured data, one of the easiest ways to do that is by marking up some of the content on your website. Chances are if you have a smaller website you are not going to break anything.

Other resources:

SEO Skeptic – one of our favorite websites for structured data and SEO in general.

SEO by the Sea – without a doubt one of the best resources for SEO patents, structured data and SEO.

Google Structured Data Testing Tool – Test your schema markup and structured data for errors and validity.

Chapter 20 - Title Tag Optimization

The title tag is the one of the simplest, yet quite possibly most important aspect of on-page SEO. The format for writing a title tag in HTML is as follows:

```
<title>Your Keyword | Name of Your Company</title>
```
or
```
<title>Key Phrase Example | Category | Name of Company</title>
```

The title of the website is not only an important factor because it is the title of that page, but it is usually what is displayed in the search results as well.

I recommend that title tags be 50-70 characters or about 512 pixels in length, which is the exact width of the Google search results.

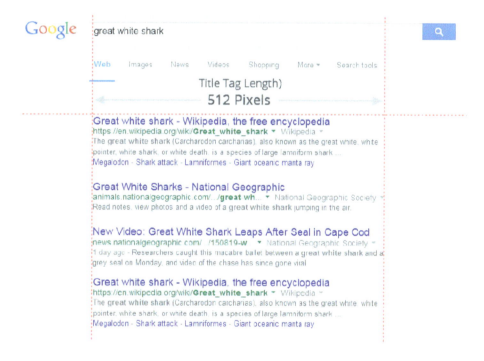

But why did SEO's start measuring title tags in pixels? In 2014 some changes were made to the search engine results page layout that really made SEO's stop and think about the way they were measuring title tags and meta descriptions. Since then, a new standard has been set and mostly all SEO's are measuring in pixels instead of characters:

Why Measure In Pixels Instead of Characters?

Both the i's and the o's are 20 characters. If we measured in characters, it would be difficult to obtain an accurate measurement.

By measuring in pixels, you can get true measurement every time

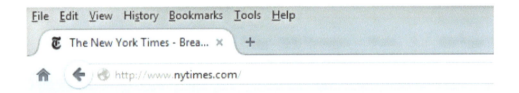

Another caveat of title tag optimization is that the title tag of a website is used by a lot of different devices, browsers, apps, and more. For instance most web browsers use the website title tag as the browser title as well. You can see in this example how even the New York Times homepage stretches beyond my browser tab.

While this isn't really a direct ranking factor for SEO, it is something to keep in mind as an internet marketer. When a visitor has 20 tabs open and they are scanning to see which one is which, you want to be able to help them find the one they are looking for. This is yet another reason to write title tags geared towards users, not search engines.

SEO Recommendations

It should go without saying that you should always try to create unique title tags for each page. Always avoid using the same title tag across multiple pages, even if you are tempted. Also just because 512 pixels is the maximum length, doesn't mean you should use it every time.

Also avoid using vague title tags such as "our homepage" or "untitled." Remember, Google tends to index pages really quickly so whatever choice you make for your title tags might be semi-permanent.

Try to put the most important keywords or the keywords you are trying to rank for at the beginning of the title tag. Several official and unofficial studies have been done on title tags that have shown the closer to the beginning that they keyword is, the more important and relevant Google considers the keyword.

Bulk Title Tag Analysis

As your website matures, I recommend doing a full title tag analysis on your website. By doing a title tag analysis on your website for SEO, it accomplishes a few things:

● \you get a good understanding of the structure of your website

● you find missing title tags

● you find incomplete or misspelled title tags

● you will find un-optimized or under-optimized title tags

Without a doubt our favorite tool for title tag analysis is Screaming Frog. Screaming Frog has a wealth of powerful features but one of our favorite features is being able to see the entire websites title tag structure at a quick glance.

Example of Title Tag Optimization

Let's take a look at an example page. In this scenario, you are an SEO working for Best Buy and your job is to write title tags for this site:

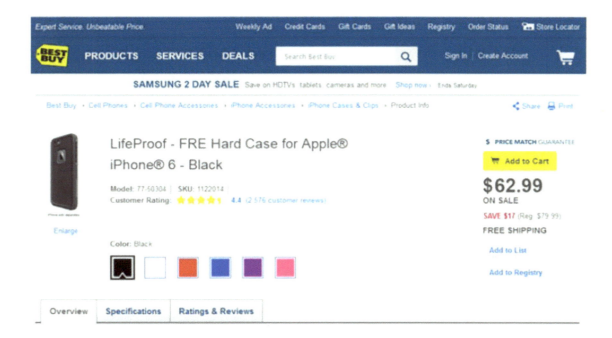

Now let's look at the title tag that displays in the search results:

Within the code, the title tag displays as such:

```
<title>LifeProof FRE Hard Case for Apple iPhone 6 Black 77-50304 -Best
Buy</title>
```

Although this title tag is only 68 characters, it is still too long for Google search results henceforth, it is truncated by Google and ended with an ellipse or "...." As an SEO, how would you handle this scenario? Would you leave the title tag the same? Is it optimized for their keyword? Are they stuffing too many keywords into it?

Really, there is no one right answer. If I polled 5 SEO's I would get 5 different answers, and all of them could theoretically be correct.

Remember SEO stands for search engine optimization, not search engine perfection. Do your best, stick to the best practices and your site will be a shining example of quality.

Other "title tags"

If you've been reading a lot of SEO tutorials in 2015 you might have come across a number of other uses of the word "title tags." Primarily the main use of this word is the

Both Facebook and Twitter have developed their own system for displaying previews within their respective social networks. In both cases they have their own "title tags" that also must be optimized and have their own specifications.

You can read more about them in our structured data section of this tutorial. Enjoy!

Chapter 21 - URL Structure and Permalinks

Creating descriptive titles, categories and taxonomies for the documents on your website will not only allow Googlebot to more efficiently crawl your website, it will help you stay organized as well. One trick about URL's I like to tell people is this: can you recite this URL over the phone without the person on the other end screwing it up?

From an SEO perspective, there are many reasons why URLs and permalinks are important. For one thing confusing URL's might be improperly linked to. A very long URL with a lot of parameters is just asking for trouble. Keywords and descriptive categories inside of your URL also might help search bots categorize and rank your site better.

This part can get a bit tricky, but is a huge part of any website. For starters a few rules of thumb:

- it is preferable to use keywords in your URL structure, but make sure it makes sense.
- stay away from complex parameters e.g. /red-bicycles is better than /?=123RB.
- use-hyphens-to-separate-words.
- underscores_are_technically_ok but can be hard to read.

If you have a static website or basic CMS or blog, this subject can be fairly simple and easy to categorize. Once you start getting into larger websites, dynamic websites and eCommerce stores is when this topic starts to get tricky. Trying to organize 1000's of products, as well as naming and categorizing them can be extremely tricky.

The real magic is when you figure out a way to optimize for both your website visitors as well as search engines. I've seen entire websites completely bomb due to their irrational and outdated URL structure.

For a lot of people this process is done during the initial website design or development process. Many people organize their page structure in a spreadsheet.

Relative vs Absolute URLs

Getting to know the difference between relative vs absolute URL's is a really important part of learning on-page SEO.

http://www.example.com/bikes.html (absolute)

bikes.html (relative)

By using absolute URLs (our preferred version) it minimizes the risk of intentionally producing duplicate content. This will also significantly reduce the amount of versions of the same URL that exist on your website.

Remember: URL's are used in search results

Like the title tag and meta description, Google uses the entire URL within the search results. This should be enough reason to ensure your URL's are properly crafted.

39 Overly Adorable Kittens To Brighten Your Day - BuzzFeed
www.buzzfeed.com/.../dont-stop-me-now-im-havin-such-a-good-time-y... ▾
Nov 4. 2014 · These kittens who threw the cutest birthday party in the universe. ... it IMPOSSIBLE for his human to leave home because he's way too cute.

Cute Kitten GIFs on Giphy
giphy.com/search/cute-kitten ▾
Search Results for Cute Kitten GIFs on Giphy. ... 855 GIFs found for cute kitten. Sort Relevant Newest · Cat Cute animated GIF cat, cute, adorable, kitten, hip hop.

Cute Kittens
cute-kittens.tumblr.com/ ▾
Cute Kitten Cat Costume. (Source: cute-kittens) Posted 3 years ago · 26 notes · Cute Kitten Cat photography Helix. (Source: cute-kittens) Posted 3 years ago.

Kittenwar! May The Cutest Kitten Win!
www.kittenwar.com/ ▾

Cute Kitten - TV Tropes
tvtropes.org/pmwiki/pmwiki.php/Main/CuteKitten ▾
The Cute Kitten trope as used in popular culture. ... Admit it, how long did you spend looking at the picture to the right before you started reading this. .

Wording your URL's

There are a lot of rules to remember when wording or describing your URL's. A few key pointers:

- stay away from stop words such as a, an, or, the, it, etc
- use descriptive keywords in your URL's
- avoid using generic words like "homepage.html"
- keep most filenames under 10-20 characters

There are a lot of rules to follow when it comes to URL's. Lucky for most SEO's is most modern day CMS's take the guess work out of creating the overall page hierarchy, most SEO's and webmasters just have to worry about naming conventions and details.

A word on breadcrumbs

A breadcrumb is technically considered part of the navigation system of the website. Breadcrumbs allows your website visitors to navigate either back to a previous part of the site or to the home page.

The beautiful part about breadcrumbs is if you know how to structure them properly, and know how to structure your site properly Google will start using them in place of the actual URL.

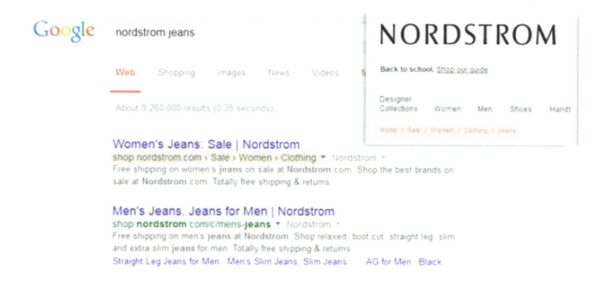

Breadcrumbs within the search results are much prettier and user friendly. Although there is no way to exactly control getting breadcrumbs in the search results, you can definitely improve your chances by simply having them. Adding structured data / semantics markup to your breadcrumbs will help Google tell what they are.

Redirects

This is another tricky and controversial topic. There comes a time in the life of a website where a page might have to be directed. This could be as a result of a change in the site structure, a 404, the merging of two pages, or a number of different reasons.

In short, redirection is when you forward one URL (website address) to another URL. Redirects can be useful for websites that change an address of a URL or another resources. Technically speaking there are different types of redirects, however most of them really accomplish the same thing from a user perspective.

As I've already said at the start of this section, there are two main types of redirects: 301 redirects and 302 redirects.

To illustrate, here is how a 301 redirect would look. This code would generally be inserted in the last line of the .htaccess file on a Linux server:

Redirect 301 /feed.xml/ http://www.elite-strategies.com/feed/

Redirect 302 /something/ http://www.example.com/somewhere-else/

Basically what this is saying "if someone tries to access feed.xml, take them instead to /feed"

If you want to see your redirects "working" you can just enter the URL in your web browser. If you want to take it a bit farther you can open up an Linux command line and use the "curl" command to grab the link.

```
HTTP/1.1 301 Moved Permanently ←
Date: Sun, 23 Aug 2015 21:09:05 GMT
Server: Apache/2.2.29 (Unix) mod_ssl/2.2.29 OpenSSL/0.9
ted/1.4
Location: http://www.elite-strategies.com/blog
Cache-Control: max-age=777600
Expires: Tue, 01 Sep 2015 21:09:05 GMT
Vary: Accept-Encoding
Connection: close
Content-Type: text/html; charset=iso-8859-1
```

```
HTTP/1.1 302 Found ←
Date: Sun, 23 Aug 2015 21:05:55 GMT
Server: Apache/2.2.29 (Unix) mod_ssl/2.2.29 OpenSSL/0.9.
ted/1.4
Location: http://www.elite-strategies.com/services
Cache-Control: max-age=777600
Expires: Tue, 01 Sep 2015 21:05:55 GMT
Vary: Accept-Encoding
Connection: close
Content-Type: text/html; charset=iso-8859-1
```

One a Windows / IIS server its done a little differently, but the overall principle is the same.

In general most qualities of that page will be passed on to the new page such as Google PageRank, "link juice" and traffic value. I'm not going to get into too much more on how to implement a redirect, as there can be many different options and configurations depending on your needs, your website, and your server. Note that even if you do redirect the page, it might take some time for Googlebot to notice. But how do you decide where to redirect your page?

This is where you'll have to make some decisions. Let's say you have a page on your website called "helpful tips" and that page has been redirect. Where do you want your users to go? What if there is no replacement for that page?

As a general rule of thumb, you should always try to redirect your users to a page that is the most relevant. If that page is not relevant you can always point them to your website sitemap (not your XML sitemap) or a category page.

302 Redirects

A 302 redirect, or temporary redirect is implemented when you want to redirect a web page for a short period of time. As a rule of thumb you should only implement a 302 when you know you are going to be removing it at some point. An example of a 302 redirect instance would be when you have a page that you want to test, or a landing page that you are trying out. Like 301's, 302's also pass PageRank and "link juice" so keep that in mind when you are creating them.

Chapter 22: XML and Website Sitemap

Think of your XML sitemap as a suggested driving directions for when Google crawls your website. Google is going to crawl your website regardless of if you have a sitemap or not, but having one will help optimize Googlebot's time on your website. You can also identify which pages are the biggest priority, and which ones change the most. For instance if you have a "jobs" page that updates frequently, you would want Google to crawl that page much more often than you would your "about us" page which probably never changes.

If you are a WordPress user there are countless plugins that can create an XML sitemap for you. Same goes for other frameworks such as Joomla, Prestashop, etc. Very rarely will you have to actually create a sitemap on your own, but if you do there are a number of tools out there that will do this for you.

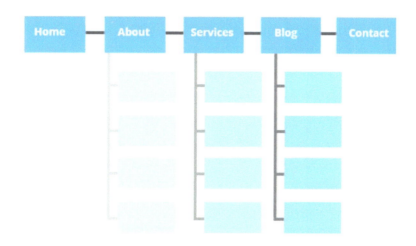

But what if you don't have a CMS such as WordPress or modern day web framework. Well, there are a few options. The first one is to build it manually and write the XML by hand. You'd do this by making a list of all of your pages from within your website, and following this format:

Example XML Sitemap Snippet

```
<url>
<loc>http://www.example.com/mypage</loc><br>
<lastmod>2013-10-10</lastmod><br>
<changefreq>monthly</changefreq><br>
<priority>1</priority><br>
</url>
```

If you don't have the patience for this, you can use a program such as Screaming Frog SEO Spider to scrape your entire website and generate the sitemap for you. It is basically a 4 step process:

1. scrape your website using Screaming Frog

2. export your XML sitemap to your computer

3. verify your XML sitemap file for errors

4. upload your sitemap to your server

Letting Google Know About Your XML Sitemap

Once you've got an XML sitemap generated and uploaded to your server, it is generally a good idea to inform Google about this. Sure, they can probably find out on their own but this is recommended. The first way to let Google know about your XML sitemap is to add your sitemap to Google Search Console (formerly Google Webmaster Tools). This is generally a 1 step process and only takes a moment if you are logged in. Once your sitemap has been added you can see all kinds of nifty stats about your website:

Another way to let Google know about your sitemap is by adding it to your robots.txt file. This is generally one line of code that looks like this:

Sitemap: http://www.example.com/sitemap.xml

If you have multiple sitemaps you can just repeat that line as many times as necessary, changing the values of course.

XML Image and Video Sitemaps

If you've gotten the concept of a regular XML sitemap that you'll have no problems understanding XML image and video sitemaps. These sitemaps are created for websites that have a lot of videos and images that typically have complex hierarchies. For instance a large website such as Vimeo that is almost completely made up of videos should have a video sitemap.

Having a specific type of sitemap also tells Google what your content is exactly. Having a video sitemap for instance will help Google give you a video snippet within the search results, but no guarantees ever.

Google has recommended in the past not only creating an XML sitemap for search engine crawlers, but to create a website map for users as well. I'll talk a little bit more about that in our next section.

Website Sitemap

To clear things up, yes there is a difference between a website sitemap. As an example here is the difference between our XML sitemap and our website or user sitemap. The XML sitemap is meant for bots, the website or user sitemap is meant for people.

The user sitemap is useful for a number of reasons. For starters, it gives your visitors a map in case they aren't sure where they are or what they are looking for. From an SEO perspective that is helpful for a number of reasons. It not only creates a perfect internal link structure, but it helps keep visitors on your site longer as well.

Google recommends a user sitemap for users that are having difficulty locating pages within your website, but a sitemap shouldn't always be an afterthought. I recommend that people looking to develop or design a new website considers designing their sitemap in a program such as Excel or Visio in the beginning, especially for larger websites. This way you can get a visual representation of how your website hierarchy looks instead of just making a good guess.

The New York Times has an absolutely exquisite website sitemap. With a website this big, they can't have every page ever written linked within the page, so they provide a basic "site map" for their users. Since they have content daying back to 1851, they are in a bit of a different category than most of the web.

Sites smaller than the NYT but larger than most like Apple makes their website sitemap a bit different. Instead of listing every link from within their website, they link to every section of the website or every category.

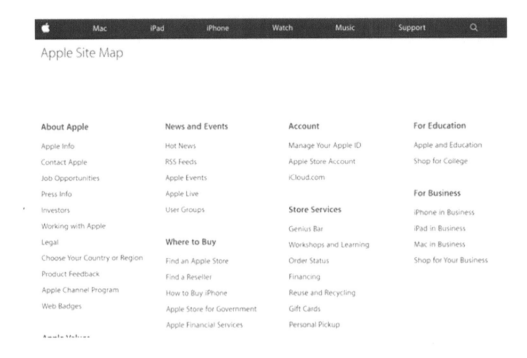

Apple Site Map

About Apple

Apple Info
Contact Apple
Job Opportunities
Press Info
Investors
Working with Apple
Legal
Choose Your Country or Region
Product Feedback
Apple Channel Program
Web Badges

Apple Values

News and Events

Hot News
RSS Feeds
Apple Events
Apple Live
User Groups

Where to Buy

Find an Apple Store
Find a Reseller
How to Buy iPhone
Apple Store for Government
Apple Financial Services

Account

Manage Your Apple ID
Apple Store Account
iCloud.com

Store Services

Genius Bar
Workshops and Learning
Order Status
Financing
Reuse and Recycling
Gift Cards
Personal Pickup

For Education

Apple and Education
Shop for College

For Business

iPhone in Business
iPad in Business
Mac in Business
Shop for Your Business

You may not think that sitemaps get visited by most users, but give it a try for a few months and see for yourself. On most websites I manage I see quite a lot of traffic going to these pages, especially ones with complex navigation.